RELIGION AND ETHICS AT ODDS

STUDIES IN JAPANESE PHILOSOPHY

Takeshi Morisato, *General Editor*

Religion and Ethics at Odds

A Buddhist Counter-Position

SUEKI FUMIHIKO

Translated by
Anton Luis Sevilla

CHISOKUDŌ

Originally published as 『反・仏教学：仏教 vs. 倫理』(Tokyo: Chikuma Shobō, 2013), a revision of 『仏教 vs. 倫理』(Tokyo: Chikuma Shobō, 2006)

Cover design: Claudio Bado

ISBN: 978-4-9907838-3-9

Nagoya, Japan
http://ChisokudoPublications.com

Contents

Translator's Introduction

Prof. Sueki Fumihiko is a towering figure in Buddhist studies in Japan. I first met him in 2010, as I was applying to take doctoral studies at the International Research Center for Japanese Studies in Kyoto. With a slight frame, a warm smile, and a gentle laugh—I would slowly learn that he laughs a whole lot—we talked about my plans to do research on Buddhist ethics. Little did I know that four years after, I would spend the last year of my doctorate translating his Buddhist critique of ethics.

Allow me to briefly introduce Prof. Sueki. He was born in Yamanashi Prefecture in 1949. He earned his undergraduate degree in Indian philosophy (Buddhism) from the University of Tokyo, studying under many of the big names in Buddhist studies, including Nakamura Hajime (author of *Ways of Thinking of Eastern Peoples*). He eventually earned his Ph.D. from the same university with a dissertation on Buddhist thought in the early Heian period. From 1995 to 2009, he was the professor of the prestigious Chair of Japanese Buddhist History in the same university.

During the 1990s, he focused on philological works, publishing books on early Japanese Buddhism, *The Blue Cliff Record* (a well-known book of Zen kōan), Kamakura Buddhism, Nichiren, etc. Until today, his books remain important texts for any aspiring Buddhist scholar in Japan.

With the opening of the twenty-first century, having laid this foundation in Buddhist studies, he turned to the task of understanding Japanese modernity vis-à-vis Buddhist tradition. He published a three-volume series on "Modern Japanese Thought: A Reconsideration." During this back and forth between the history of thought and

Buddhist studies, glimmers of a completely novel perspective to philosophy began to appear in his thought.

Halfway through the first decade of the twenty-first century, he was ready to take on philosophy and contemporary issues head-on. The first of these explicitly philosophical books was this book, *Religion and Ethics at Odds*. It was first entitled *Buddhism vs. Ethics* when it was published in 2006. The book remains in print, and has been re-published as *Anti-Buddhology: Buddhism vs. Ethics* in 2013—a testament to its continued importance. Since the publication of this book, Prof. Sueki has continued to develop his philosophy, publishing books like *The Other, the Dead, the I* (2007) and *Philosophy Live: A Perspective from Japan* (2012), the latter soon to be available in English translation. (Prof. Sueki gives a detailed first-person account of the development of his thought in the addendum of this book. He also gives an extensive listing of his books and the role they play in this new philosophy.)

In 2009, he moved to the Nichibunken in Kyoto. I would meet him shortly after, and would study with him until his retirement in 2015. He is chair of the Japanese Association for Comparative Philosophy (originally started by Nakamura Hajime) and continues to develop his philosophy of the other/dead, adding yearly to his long list (almost 30 self-authored, and more co-authored, edited, and translated volumes) of publications. He is truly a giant in this field.

Ethics and trans-ethics

As one can see above, this book shows the beginnings of Prof. Sueki's philosophical thought—a philosophy built on a firm foundation of rigorous philology of Buddhist texts and careful scrutiny of the intellectual history of Japan. However, the value of the publication of this work in English is not merely academic, nor merely for those interested in Japanese studies. There are two main issues—contemporary, global, *human* issues—that I think this book addresses:

First, this book addresses the *limits* of ethics. Second, this book focuses on the problem of the other / dead.

Let us begin with the first issue. This is probably the first thing that gets people scratching their heads about this book. Why does Prof. Sueki keep criticizing ethics? As a specialist in ethics, this question was particularly confounding for me.

One cultural issue here is the gap between "ethics" in English and *rinri* in Japanese. "Ethics" has a very broad range of connotations: It refers to moral principles (good vs. evil) held by an individual, or by a group. It can be time-bound or timeless. It can be particular or universal. Thus the phrase "ethical people" can refer to those who abide by the rules, or the opposite—those who criticize social rules as erroneous conventions. For example, if we take moral education as the trumpet of ethics, the famed psychologist and ethicist Lawrence Kohlberg includes pre-conventional (egoist), conventional (group-based), and post-conventional (critical) morality in the definition of morality, and sets the post-conventional stage as the most developed form of morality.

The Japanese *rinri* is a completely different story. *Rinri*, more than anything, refers to the moral principles of a group—particular, time-bound principles. Thus agitators and social critics do *not* generally fit within this category. And moral education in Japan has much more conventional undertones than Kohlberg—especially in light of Japanese wartime moral education (*shūshin*), which tended to subjugate individuals to the totality. And so while criticizing ethics is shocking in English, criticizing *rinri* in Japanese is, while shocking, somewhat understandable in a post-war context.

However, Prof. Sueki's critique of *rinri* goes beyond the critique of conventional morality. He is not merely a social critic advocating for post-conventional morality and social re-construction. In this book, the word "ethics" accrues the meaning of "rules or principles that govern human relations." Ethics is the *order* between people *as orderable*. This definition applies to conventional morality, but it also applies to rational post-conventional morality (like Jürgen Habermas' discourse ethics). Ethics refers to the ground we can stand on—be it reason or feeling or identity or rights—from which we can say, "this, for sure, is good."

Against this, Prof. Sueki introduces the term "trans-ethics" (*chō-rinri*). This is not merely about going beyond conventions and creating new conventions. It is about recognizing that no matter how much we expand the realm of order, this sure footing of ethics is *finite*—it has boundaries, and beyond it, there is no certainty about good and evil.

Recently, with issues in political ethics, environmental ethics, bioethics, information ethics, and ethics in education, there has been a resurgence in interest in Buddhist ethics. Different ideas in Buddhism—and their resonance with fields like psychology and neuroscience—have been found to be helpful guides in our attempt to build better lives—better relationships with ourselves, each other, and our world. However, perhaps we can take Prof. Sueki's point as a pointed question: Is this all there is to Buddhism? Is Buddhism merely about being good, and having sure footing in that goodness? (This applies not just to Buddhism but to religion/spirituality in general.)

Perhaps, in our necessary attempt to redirect our lives toward the good, we have become too attached to the idea of ethics, seeing it as limitless. This book does not seek to belittle ethics—this world has both too little and too much ethics. Rather than belittle ethics, perhaps this book only seeks to put ethics in its place.

THE OTHER/DEAD

Why is it that we need to go beyond the ethical? Prof. Sueki's key argument is that each and every one of us has to deal with this trans-ethical realm because we are in relation with the *other*. Relating with one who cannot be reduced to the orders of comprehension, we are forced into a world where reason and order no longer hold sway. This is the second issue he raises: the importance of the idea of the other/dead.

In the English-speaking world, Buddhism and postmodernity always had a sort of affinity for each other. The realization of the limits of reason and the rational subject seems to resonate with the Buddhist focus on no-self, particularly on the Zen Buddhist idea of truth "not depending on words and letters" that crossed over to the West through Buddhist ambassadors like D. T. Suzuki and Izutsu Toshihiko.

However, as any Zen Buddhist "fan" realizes when visiting Japan, actual Japanese Buddhism is a whole different animal from the philosophical mysticism we read about in philosophy books. Here in Japan, there is a much greater concern for funerals than there is for Zen meditation, and more ceremonies for the repose of souls than there are expressions of "no-self." Furthermore, postmodernity, particularly poststructuralists like Emmanuel Levinas and Jacques Derrida, focus on the notion of the otherness (alterity) of the other—an idea that seems weak both in Japanese traditional thought and in the practice of Buddhism.

In light of this, what Prof. Sueki presents in this book is none other than a re-encounter between Japanese Buddhism and the postmodern idea of the other. But unlike the intellectual / philosophical Buddhism of the ambassadors of Buddhism in the 60s, his Buddhism is a Buddhism of the everyday person. It focuses on the real representative of Japanese Buddhism—the much denigrated "funeral Buddhism"— with its confusing mix of Buddhist, Shintoist, and even western modernist ideas.

What Prof. Sueki derives from this funeral Buddhism, however, is a unique approach to the face of the other. While including both postmodern and even psychoanalytic approaches to alterity, he focuses on the real, undeniable experience of *loss*. Experiencing the loss of a loved one means experiencing a relationship that is real, but that is no longer within the orders of reason and brute existence. And it is this experience that brings us beyond the world of ethics, into the world of the trans-ethical.

I entrust the development of these ideas to the rest of this book. Here, allow me to merely repeat my assertion: This book is not merely an academic engagement of Japanese Buddhism. By engaging the problem of the limits of ethics and the problem of the other/dead, it gives us a new philosophy, a novel approach as we wrestle with the new problems of this truly postmodern age.

This world needs ethics. This world needs us to recognize the people we are connected to. But at the same time, the world needs more than just ethics. And there is more to relationships than recognition. It is difficult to walk the narrow path between attachment to and rejection of ethics. I hope this translation might offer insights to those who are trying to walk this path, in various parts of the globe.

Anton Luis Sevilla
September 2016

Preface to the English Edition

In this book, I take the standpoint of Japanese Buddhism and examine issues specific to Japan, like funeral Buddhism and the bombing of Hiroshima, as philosophical problems. This book therefore considers the problems of philosophy, ethics, and religion from an angle completely different from prior thought in America and Europe. I have been conducting philological research on Japanese Buddhism for many years now, and I wanted to test out how useful these unique ideas might be for addressing contemporary issues.

Given this, I am not very confident about how universalizable my ideas are. However, considering how occidental thought has hit an impasse of sorts, I wonder if it might be useful to consider various radically different approaches like the one I present. In *Intimacy or Integrity: Philosophy and Cultural Difference* (2002), Thomas Kasulis argues that Japanese thought is more intimacy-oriented than integrity-oriented. In this vein, one could say that my book tries to develop the notion of intimacy further. In particular, the problem of the dead in part two has yet to be sufficiently discussed—even in Japan—and my book was one of the first to take this up philosophically.

At first, the Japanese version of this book was published serially in a magazine for Buddhist monks entitled *The Prosperity of Temples*. This source material was completely reworked and republished by Chikuma Shobō as a paperback, *Buddhism vs. Ethics*. (See the afterword for details.) In 2013, an expanded edition was published with the title *Anti-Buddhology: Buddhism vs. Ethics*. This edition was to be the basis for the present English translation. The appendix of this book was added in 2013, and is not merely an appendix but a summary of the development of my thought from 2006 to 2013. I would much appreciate it if you gave it a look.

I asked Anton Luis Sevilla, who was in the process of writing his dissertation, to translate this book, with the support of JSPS Kakenhi Grant 24520096. The Japanese version of this book was not an academic piece but something like a free essay written in conversational Japanese. Anton quite skillfully translated this into easygoing English prose. We printed 100 copies and gave it to anyone interested, and it was quite well-received. It caught the eye of James Heisig and Morisato Takeshi of the Nanzan Institute of Religion and Culture, and I am very pleased that they have agreed to publish it through Chisokudō's new format. I fervently hope that this book inspires new discussions and debates in the fields of philosophy, ethics, and religion.

Sueki Fumihiko 末木文美士
September 2016

Why I Dislike Ethics

Now I have to think about ethics for the next 30 chapters. How do I even begin? In the first place, am I even qualified to talk about ethics? To be honest, I have a real distaste for ethics, morality, or anything of the sort. Even now, when I hear those words, it makes me feel a little ill. Come to think of it, we had a subject called "Ethics and Society" back when I was in high school. I never took it seriously, and I do not recall ever listening to it attentively. Well, I was also at an age when I was overflowing with cheekiness.

It would be wonderful if children could be raised up well just through moral education. But if one wants to know what happens when children buy into moral education completely, prewar Japanese society gives a ready example. Unfortunately, there are quite a few "adults" who would love to have a repeat of that.

Because of this, ethics and morals have been my enemies. And because I have been vocal about this on various occasions, people frown upon me and refuse to keep my company. When I spoke about this at a research conference, there was a person who harshly countered, saying, "Then how do *you* think about social responsibility?" But does it suffice to take carrying out our "social responsibilities" as our final *telos*? To put it bluntly, is that any different from the repulsive wartime phrase "extinguishing the self in public service" (*messhi hōkō*) or the notion of the "company's man" that was in vogue during the period of Japan's rapid economic growth?

When I was young, I had not really thought this through. But nevertheless, I decided to specialize not in ethics but in religion. Religion exists in a tensional relationship with ethics. While ethical religion is possible, that would be no more than one facet of religion. And to say the least, it is in the part irreducible to ethics where the true problem of religion lies. But it is difficult to even define "religion." I will touch on that a bit more, later on.

THE DOMAIN OF RELIGION

In some ways, the world of religion is a peculiar one. It includes things like religious sensitivities and experiences, which are not shared by all human beings. There are parts of this world that those who grasp it do, and those who do not, do not. Despite that, the problem that religion presents has a universal meaning, which transcends the question of whether or not an individual has these religious sensitivities or experiences. Of course, this could be said of other fields and is not a problem peculiar to religion. For instance, science has this generally accepted idea, or *tatemae*, that in theory anyone can understand science. But by no means does that imply that anyone can make scientific discoveries—that would require special talent.

Some might say that if the existence of the domain of religion depended on religious sensitivities and experiences, then it would just be a matter of saying (for those who have religious sensitivities) that there is a domain called "the religious," and nothing more. "Modernity" has constantly belittled religion. People thought of religion as a mere superstition of sorts, thinking that it would someday wither away with the progress of science. They thought that the world would more likely be at peace if religion ceased to exist. However, is that how things really are? Today, the limits of both science and ethics have been completely exposed. Now, what then?

I do not intend to fixate on the word "religion." If one feels uncomfortable with this word, there is no need to use it at all. All I wish to say is that there are problems that cannot be explained away by ethics, science, politics, economics, or law. Perhaps the true problems of humanity lie at the very point where we deviate from that domain of rationality. Objectively speaking, until now, it is what we call "religion" that has most deeply involved itself with these kinds of problems. And so when dealing with such problems that are irreducible to ethics and science, I do not think it is a bad idea to make use of religion.

However, I have no plans on preaching or sharing my religious experiences. Rather, I would like to theoretically clarify the domain that religion investigates, and do so in accordance with language. Perhaps such an undertaking would be closest to the field we call "philosophy" (*tetsugaku*). Please allow me to refer to it as such.

Buddhism as a Methodology

The field I have been involved in as a researcher is not religion in general, nor philosophy, but rather the study of a particular religion—Buddhism. The scope of my knowledge and powers of thinking is quite narrow. Why did I end up with Buddhism? I am afraid I lack a particularly profound reason for that. As an ordinary Japanese person, I simply had more moments where I felt affinity to Buddhism, rather than to Christianity or Islam.

At university, as I wrestled with philosophy, something struck me as quite odd. All the discussions were about the west, and when speaking about religion, people always seemed to presuppose Christianity as a model. Not only that, people spoke of Christianity as if it possessed some sort of "universality." To be honest, that did not quite fit with my sensibilities, and I began to doubt if I could keep learning a "philosophy" like that.

If I am to learn philosophy, might it not be better if I take Buddhism, which is nearest to me, as my point of departure, and think about the problem of my own way of life from there? In my youth, I agonized over this quite a lot, eventually deciding to go into Buddhist studies. Back then, it was thought strange for a good young lad, like me, to study Buddhism (given that I was not born to a temple family), and I was treated like an oddity. Well there is truth in that, for sure.

The academic field that does research on Buddhism is referred to as "Buddhist studies." In this field, for the most part, one does not deal directly with contemporary problems. Rather, one patiently immerses oneself in the study of classical texts. One has to have a knack for things like these. For a person like me, who was completely sick of dealing with the people around and the savage realities of the present, there was no better world possible. I was absorbed in that world for 30 years.

After 30 years, I came to and looked around me—and became anxious once again. The world of the classics used to be the place where I could be most at peace, but I began to realize that this feeling could not last. No matter how hard I might try to cover it up, I live in the present, and there is no real way to escape from that. The idea of a comfort zone where one can be okay all by oneself is a myth, nothing more. Also, Buddhism does not exist merely in the literature of the past, but rather, functions in the present. If so, there is really no way to escape from the problems of the contemporary world. If we call such a standpoint from which one studies Buddhism "contemporary Buddhist studies," then perhaps it is necessary for us to establish such a field against the conventional field of "classical Buddhist studies."

Because of this, what unfolds in this book is, in a way, an attempt at contemporary Buddhist studies. However, I do not intend to be particularly caught up with Buddhism. Buddhism is a handhold, a means and not an end in itself. I call this "Buddhism as a methodology."

It would be a waste to overlook that which remains of the deep way of thinking left for me by the ancestors of Japan. Moreover, the tradition accumulated by my ancestors lies in the depths of Japanese culture and continues to shape the way Japanese people think. Would an elucidation of Buddhist thinking not be simultaneously an elucidation of my own depths? Why should I imitate the philosophy of the west, when it is alien and ill-fitting for me? The founding spirit of western philosophy is "Know thyself." Ironically, it is quite the opposite of what philosophers do these days (especially in Japan).

This book does not presuppose that Buddhism is correct or anything of the sort. I assure you, there are many elements in Buddhism that ought to be criticized. I have no intention to develop an apologetics. In this book, I shall take up various problems that ethics and morality are no longer able to deal with, and think about them from the standpoint of someone who has studied Buddhism. In the process, I shall simultaneously criticize tradition and disassemble (or deconstruct) it.

Previously, some philosophers went off saying that if the west is no good, well, there is the "east." They argued for the "overcoming of western modernity," and they put the profundity of eastern philosophy in its place, singing the latter's praises. Of all things, it is that "wonderful" but dangerous glorification of Japan and the east that should be thoroughly criticized. I argue that there is no other way to build a philosophy that can stand on its own feet than by coming to terms with oneself in a critical way.

In this book, I would like to lay the foundations for my argument in Part One (Chapters 1 to 9) by reflecting on the history of Buddhist thought and taking up the problems in the relationship between Buddhism and ethics. I think I can get some foothold through this, in order to proceed more surely. Then, I will argue with a greater sense of generality. In Part Two (Chapters 10 to 20), the argument will revolve around the problem of the "other"[1] that transcends the ethical world (the latter I refer to as the domain of *human beings* or *ningen*). And in Part Three (Chapters 21 to 30) I will raise the issue of whether we can open a new way of thinking by considering our relationship with the dead (who can rightfully be considered as the most other of others).

1. [The word "other" has a somewhat Levinasian tone. As such, it is generally kept in the singular and not attached to articles ("an other" instead of "another"). However, we will not adhere to the post-structural intricacies of differentiating "other" and "Other," and will simply keep it in lower case.]

In the very place that transcends ethics lie problems that we truly need to contend with. We can call this domain the *trans-ethical*.[2] I do not know how many people will be willing to accept my farfetched ideas. But today, it is no longer possible to glorify life, as a living being, while ignoring the dead. What I hope to suggest is not a foolish optimism, nor a reckless pessimism, but for us to descend into the very depths of ourselves, and from there ascertain if something might come to life.

2. [*Chō-rinri* is one of the key words of this book. *Chō* indicates going beyond: "trans" or "super." It shall be translated as "trans-ethical" or "trans-ethics."]

Part One

Putting Buddhism into Question

1

Dubious Matters:
Buddhism and Ethics

Despite being a specialist of Buddhism, because of the things I just mentioned, my declarations can seem suspect to others. "Serious" Buddhists have often complained about the things I say. I met a Buddhist monk who had come from Korea to study in Japan. He once asked me, "Sensei, do you *really* believe in Buddhism?" The question was so direct, almost accusatory, that a part of me cringed. He was a very serious sort of person, and I hear he has been doing great things in Buddhist circles since his return home. I am sure from his perspective it was hard to put up with a person like me, who had nothing but bad things to say about Buddhism.

I answered him by saying, "Well it depends on what you mean by 'Buddhism' and what you mean by 'believe.'" It might seem like I was dodging the question, but no, I was being honest. Because Buddhism has no conditions for faith, unlike Christianity, there is no objective basis to determine whether or not one "believes in Buddhism." Could we call the organized Buddhism of the present day "Buddhism?" If yes, then I would have to say quite frankly, I could not possibly believe in a Buddhism of that sort.

So, what *is* Buddhism? Fairly recently, some researchers raised the question of what a "correct Buddhism" might be. It turned into a huge debate—what is called the "Critical Buddhism" movement. I myself got caught up in that debate, and I shall discuss this in greater detail at another time. But one can see from the course of this movement that "correct Buddhism" is not something with an objective standard, but rather depends on the subjective way of being of the person who practices it. In other words, it does not depend on any existing authorities, but is a matter of seeing with one's own eyes, feeling with one's own heart, and thinking with one's own head. If one could carry that out, it would be a marvelous thing. I would like to, at the very least, strive in that direction.

"Śākyamuni said such and such—oh isn't Buddhism wonderful?" I would never preach like that. Buddhism should not be exempted from scrutiny. Considering this, then, rather than the standpoint of religion, where one enters via faith, it is the path of philosophy, where one enters via doubt, which is dearer to me. From the eyes of those who possess a strong faith, this might seem terribly imprudent, if not outright blasphemous against Buddhism. But I begin with the idea that if something is not believable, there is no point in forcing oneself to believe.

On the Right to Speak of Ethics and Morality

Let us return to the problem of ethics. Previously, there was a time when there was a spike in the number of heinous crimes committed by the youth, which caused a great commotion in Japan. Back then, a young boy asked "But why shouldn't we kill people?" And everyone flew into a frenzy, coming out with special editions of magazines about his question, debating on television, quibbling about theories, and otherwise making fools of themselves. It was somewhat strange. Throughout history, the questions of the youth have not changed much. I wrestled with the same question when I was in middle school, and I have carried those doubts with me ever since.

It is not that we are outright forbidden from killing people. The samurai took killing as their profession. And even now, war is about people killing each other. Then perhaps one would say that war itself is wrong. I am a coward, so I terribly dislike war. But even if I dislike it, there are times when one must fight. For example, can we criticize the Buddhists who supported the war of resistance of the Chinese against Japan, when the Japanese invaded them, and say they are "war supporters?" Can we really say that they betrayed the spirit of Buddhism by failing to be thoroughly pacifist? I do not think so.

When 9/11 occurred and America waged a war of retribution in Afghanistan, some Buddhists in Japan said something to the effect that Americans ought to take Gandhi's spirit of non-violence. Frankly, such a sentiment seemed too far up in the clouds. Anyone can look on from the outside and prattle about non-violence and anti-war sentiment.

However, is there any resolve behind this? If Japan were to organize in full support of an all-out war, would one be able to maintain this non-violent anti-war position? If one were under observation by the Special Higher Police, criticized on all fronts as a "red" and a "traitor," captured and tortured—perhaps even then, taking it all on as an individual, one might still be able to carry on. But if one's family also came under attack—"mother of a traitor," "son of a red"—forced to spend their days miserable and cast out, would one still be able to maintain this non-violent anti-war stance?

That is what Gandhi demands of us—not sitting comfortably on an armchair, criticizing people from a distance. Rather, he demands a struggle that stakes one's life and is willing to sacrifice even one's family and friends. On that point, it was no different from the anti-Japanese resistance of Chinese Buddhists. The question is whether people are capable of that or not.

Honestly, I am not strong enough for that. Although I may despise war, although I may despise murder, I am not strong enough to withstand torture and sacrificing my family in order to hold fast to my beliefs. Inwardly, I would probably grumble, but outwardly, I would follow the lead of society and country. Perhaps I will be told that this "If you can't beat 'em, join 'em" sort of attitude won't do. But I know, better than anyone else, that I am not strong enough to resist. And because of this, I do not have the right to talk about ethics or morality. I do not have the *strength* to talk about ethics and morality.

My former Professor in graduate school, Tamura Yoshirō, was a strong believer in *The Lotus Sutra*. When students were being sent to the front, he was drafted into the military, and his superior asked him, "What is superior, the emperor or *The Lotus Sutra*?" He said he had no choice but to reply, "The emperor." Had he said, "*The Lotus Sutra* is superior," that would have been *lèse-majesté* and he would have been in dire straits for that. He told us over and over again how his deep shame over that episode spurred him on in academia.

Nobody can blame him for having replied that way. But he did not shelf that episode, then go on preaching ethics and morality after the war. Rather, all his life he bore a sense of reproach toward this (perhaps inevitable) act and turned that into the driving force of his academic efforts. I think we can see my *sensei*'s sincerity there. When I heard this story, I began to feel that I could really depend on this teacher.

CASTING DOUBT ON MORALISM AND ETHICS-CENTRISM

Perhaps it is only when "rightness" is frustrated by antinomy, when one realizes that one cannot maintain one's course within the ethical, and when one starts to ask, "Is ethical 'rightness' really all there is?" that for the first time, a new world dawns upon us. It was from this standpoint that a group of Buddhists criticized the moralism of the Meiji period (1868–1912). During this time, the Meiji constitution had just been established, and a state centered on the emperor was set up, backed by the promulgation of the Imperial Rescript on Education (1890). With this, the principles of the morality of the nation were put in place. That was the beginning of the era of ethics and morality. People had freedom of religion, but everyone had to adhere to the morality centered on the emperor. Thus, morality was superior to religion. This was how things were back then.

In the midst of that, there were Buddhists who challenged the foundationality of the ethics and morality of the secular world: Kiyozawa Manshi of the True Pure Land school, and the Nichirenist, Takayama Chogyū. Frustrated by this fixation on ethics and morality, they criticized this standpoint and thus opened the way to religion. People criticized them heavily, demanding, "How then do you think of society and the state?" But as they both died early from tuberculosis, they sadly left us with answers that are less than sufficient.

Recently, I have been drawn to issues like these and have put myself to work on them. I will likely pick this up again later on in this book. In any case, it is very important—and very encouraging—that Buddhists have criticized moralism and taken an attitude of pursuing religion beyond ethics and morality.

And so I would like to take a critical skepticism toward both Buddhism and ethics as my point of departure. Anyone can spout fine things about ethics. "Let's value life and nature! Buddhism is a religion that values life and religion." Sure, one can tout slogans like these, but when asked what we actually have to do, or what we actually can do, how does one answer? It is not a matter of talk but of what one can actually carry out. It is wise to question that sort of fancy talk.

But if one criticizes ethics, will that not make life in human society impossible? Is that not tantamount to anomie, to lawlessness? Is that not completely irresponsible? These attacks come up quite naturally in response to my approach. Of course, there is a domain in which ethics does function quite well. But it is necessary to clarify from where ethics is established and where its limits lie. The point of this book is to try to organize my thoughts in a way that lets me accomplish that task.

That being said, we must not get ahead of ourselves. I would like to start with a brief analysis of the history of Buddhism's engagement with ethics. My fundamental stance is that the present stands atop the accumulation of the past. Therefore, without properly getting a handhold on the past, there is no way to address our contemporary issues.

2

Buddhism's Lack of Ethicality

Tamura Yoshirō delved deeply into the problem of Buddhism and ethics. One of the results of this is his article, "The Problem of the Lack of Ethicality in Buddhism."[1] Here, rather than speaking of Buddhist ethics as self-evident, he takes the opposite track and considers the charge that Buddhism lacks ethics. He also discusses the basis on which this is argued, and whether or not such an argument makes sense. No matter how many times I read this article, it seems fresh to me. And I must confess, every time I think of taking up the problem of ethics and trace his argument, I find that I am not able to bring it much further.

In this article, Tamura takes up the critique of Buddhism and religion from the standpoint spanning the anti-Buddhism of the Edo period to Inoue Tetsujirō's prioritization of secular ethics. Against this, he also takes up Kiyozawa Manshi's and other thinkers' decisive negation of ethics and morality, and the resulting securing of a standpoint particular to religion. Furthermore, he discusses the critique, this time from Christianity, that Buddhism lacks ethicality. This is contrasted with the ethicality of Christianity. Here, he writes that the ethics of Christianity is

> unlike Confucian ethics, which is an ethics of maintaining the order
> inside a closed society, but rather is something that negates and tran-

---

1. Tamura Yoshirō 田村芳朗『田村芳朗仏教学論集2・日本仏教論』[Tamura Yoshirō's collected essays on Buddhist studies], vol. 2 (Tokyo: Shunjūsha, 1991).

scends such an ethics, and from such a negation and transcendence, gives rise to the shaping of history and reformation of society.[2]

Allow me to discuss in advance some ideas that I will be taking up in Part Two of this book. Here, I will refer to the standpoint of ethics that regulates the relationships between people as "the standpoint of *ningen.*"[3]

That is because *ningen* (the characters of which literally mean "person" + "between") is "the relationship between persons." That is quite close to what Tamura referred to as "Confucian ethics, which is an ethics of maintaining the order inside a closed society." Much of the anti-Buddhism in the Confucianism of the Edo period came from such a standpoint. However, such an ethics is not necessarily limited to what is "inside closed society," but I think it can include a much wider scope—even the issues of humankind as a whole.

In contrast, one can rephrase the Christian critique as follows: Christianity transcends the standpoint of "*ningen,*" and has an ethics that is born from a higher dimension particular to religion. This is supposedly something that Buddhism lacks. In other words, while Christianity can assert a transcendent ethics rooted in God, Buddhism does not have anything that corresponds to God, and thus cannot assert a transcendent ethics founded on an absolute basis.

According to Tamura, most of the criticisms against Buddhism made by philosophers and the religious can be classified into three: the criticism of Buddhism as seclusionism, as a philosophy of emptiness and oneness, and as mysticism. By seclusionism, he means that Buddhism supposedly tends to one-sidedly stress going beyond the secular world. It therefore also tends to be apathetic toward actual problems. By the philosophy of emptiness and oneness, he is referring to the prob-

---

2. Ibid., 37.

3. [*Ningen* 人間 is usually translated as "human beings" or "a human being." I will often leave this untranslated, because it maintains the tension between the individual and plural and the notion of what is *between* persons in ways that the English words cannot.]

lem wherein if everything were empty and without substance, and thus one (one body, one likeness) in the world of *satori* (enlightenment), would it not be impossible to differentiate between good and evil? Finally, by mysticism, he is pointing to how ascribing ultimate value to the experience of *satori* comes at the price of belittling everything else.

Furthermore, Tamura points out that criticisms of this sort have been primarily directed at Buddhism's social ethics. However, he expresses his doubt, writing:

> Is it that Buddhism's fundamental standpoint lacks ethicality, as pointed above? Or is it that this [ethicality] died out in the history of its development, or due to the areas to which it was transmitted? Or are both these ideas of lack or loss mere prejudices, with [Buddhism] fully exhibiting this [ethicality]?[4]

In the end, he does not give an answer to these questions, leaving us with nothing more than hints. Tamura has thus bequeathed to us the task of seeing how to proceed from there.

In this book, I will explore this problem further. But first, let me briefly touch upon how I will develop my argument. I do not really mind if Buddhism lacks a religious, transcendent ethics akin to Christianity's. Ethics is no more than an issue of the rules of *ningen* in the secular world. But we always run up against issues that cannot be reduced to the rules of *ningen*, and it is these issues that are weightier. Transcending the mutual understanding of *ningen*, we encounter the other, particularly the most other of others—the dead. How can we take our encounter with the other and with the dead as a point of departure? This is the problem of "trans-ethics"—that, as the neologism indicates, goes beyond the domain of ethics.

Even within Buddhism, the problem of the other did not become a considerable concern in the early period. Rather, it was ethics that flourished. The other became a main issue in the idea of the Bodhi-

4. Ibid. 50–1.

sattva and in the process of the formation of Mahāyāna Buddhism. Simultaneously, this was also the process of the fall of ethics and the exodus toward the trans-ethical. However, researchers up to the present have not really looked at things this way, and because of this, it is necessary to rethink the very framework by which we grasp Buddhism.

What I am trying to carry out, however, could be said to be an extreme interpretation of Buddhism. Against this interpretation, it is certainly possible to see Buddhism and ethics as compatible with each other. Actually, that way of seeing things is more common. "Engaged Buddhism" is the phrase used to refer to social activities carried out in the spirit of Buddhist ethics, and this movement has been gaining attention of late (See Chapter 8). It is not that I disagree with movements like this, because they are, in themselves, serious attempts to rethink Buddhism's existence today. But one caveat: In such a case, ethics is still a concern within the domain of *ningen*, and is by no means a transcendental ethics, like that of Christianity.

Well, people say that the lack of ethicality in Buddhism is particularly distinct in *Japanese* Buddhism. This is the problem Tamura pointed out, about the regional character of Buddhism. In the remaining parts of this chapter, I will try to take up the tradition of the doctrine of innate enlightenment (*hongaku shisō*), which is the most representative of this Japanese Buddhist lack of ethicality.

What is the Doctrine of *Hongaku*?

Actually, Tamura was a specialist in the study of the doctrine of *hongaku*.[5] Up until then, *hongaku* theory was a field carried out by but a small fraction of researchers. It was Tamura who first grasped it as the core of Japanese Buddhism—not just an issue of a narrow portion

---

5. [*Hongaku* 本覚 is usually translated as innate, inherent, original, or originary enlightenment. To maintain the manifold meanings of this Japanese keyword, it will remain untranslated.]

of Buddhism but as a keyword to recapture the entirety of Japanese culture. Since it is a philosophy that is just coming into the spotlight, its terms and definitions are ambiguous, and it tends to stir up various debates.

Broadly defined, *hongaku* theory refers to the Buddhist thought, which developed in medieval Japan, that affirms the present reality as it is. More specifically, it refers to the trend that developed particularly during the Middle Ages in the Tendai school, and is also called Tendai *hongaku* theory. The method of oral instruction developed in the medieval Tendai school, and in that method, the ultimate truth is not publicly declared but is instead passed on behind closed doors from master to disciple. In this school, there is the *Eshin* school and the *Dāna* school, and Tendai *hongaku* theory was formed in the midst of this oral tradition. This kind of trend began during the latter part of the Heian period, developed during the middle ages, and was criticized to the point that it was driven into decline sometime in the Edo period. But despite all of that, it still left a big impact. Even though it was an oral tradition, it was gradually written down and preserved, so it is possible to look into its contents even today.

One representative book of the doctrine of *hongaku* is the *Book of Thirty-Four Articles*. Here, we find things like "Impermanence, while being impermanent, is permanent and does not pass away. Discrimination, while being discrimination, is permanent and does not pass away." And, "One cannot say that by turning sentient beings, they become the body of the Buddha. Sentient beings, while being sentient beings, and the Pure Land, while being the Pure Land, are both permanent and awakened." In other words, this impermanent world, as impermanent, realizes eternal enlightenment. There is no need to search anew for enlightenment outside of it. Sentient beings are fine as they are; they do not need to become buddhas. Hell is fine remaining as hell, and human beings are fine remaining as human beings.

From the ordinary Buddhist way of thinking, it is only by going through religious practice that one can attain enlightenment. But from *hongaku* theory's way of thinking, practice is not necessary, and the unenlightened person (*bonbu*) is fine the way he is. Also, sentient beings are not the only ones who can become buddhas; plants can become buddhas as well. Moreover, plants do not need to become buddhas. It is not a problem if plants do not attain Buddhahood. Plants that have not reached Buddhahood, remaining as they are, make up the world of Buddha.

Thus, according to the doctrine of *hongaku*, everything in this world is fine the way it is, and nothing needs to be "fixed" at all. Even though Tendai *hongaku* theory is seen as the typical example of this way of thinking, this way of thinking can also be seen outside of that. Medieval Buddhism in general can be referred to as *hongaku* theory, in the broader sense of the term. *Hongaku* theory had a big impact on medieval Japanese culture. For instance, the notion that impermanence as impermanence is fine as it is can also be seen in the *Essays on Idleness*. The idea that natural vegetation as itself already contains the world of the Buddha is also present in things like medieval entertainment and arts, the art of the tea ceremony, and the way of flower arrangement.

THE ANTI-ETHICAL CHARACTER OF THE DOCTRINE OF *HONGAKU*

However, things get difficult when it comes to questions relating to ethics. If one thought from the standpoint wherein the secular world, as it is, is the world of Buddha, one could end up completely affirming secular ethics (of *ningen*), resulting in a heavy emphasis on ethics. In the beginning of the Edo period (1603–1868), a rather peculiar Zen Buddhist named Suzuki Shōsan (1579–1655) preached that each worldly occupation in the Edo hierarchy—samurai, farmers, artisans, and merchants—in the realizing of their worldly occupations, were already doing Buddha work, in a Buddhist vocational theory of work (see Chapter 14). This could also be said to be a kind of *hongaku* philosophy. Also, in connection with ecology today, the *hongaku* idea that natural vegetation is, as itself, the world of Buddha, has been attracting attention in the field of environmental ethics (See Chapter 20).

Well then, does the doctrine of *hongaku* really emphasize secular ethics? One cannot say for sure. Another possibility is that accepting the present condition as it is can result in accepting the unenlightened person, stained with the worldly desires that give rise to suffering, as being fine as he or she is. Here, the moment for self-improvement (or spiritual elevation) is lost, and one would fall into an unprincipled and unthinking anti-ethicism, in which it does not matter what one does.

This type of argument has frequently been a problem for the followers of Hōnen and Shinran. If all were unconditionally saved by Amitābha Buddha then one would fall into the problematic notion of the "unobstructed creation of evil" wherein one could wreak whatever havoc one pleases. This kind of thinking is also deeply connected to *hongaku* thinking. The well-known theory, found in the *Lamentations of Divergences* (*Tannishō*), of the salvation of evil persons (*akunin shōki*, which states that evil people have a unique opportunity to be saved by Amitābha) was also born out of this tendency. If everything in the present world was affirmed, then wrongdoings, and the reasons why wrongs should be opposed, would all disappear.

In recent years, the Critical Buddhism movement intensely criticized the anti-ethical nature of the doctrine of *hongaku*. Critical Buddhism originated from Sōtō Buddhist scholars Hakamaya Noriaki and Matsumoto Shirō, who have brought forth severe criticisms against traditional Buddhist studies. Its influence has even spread considerably outside Japan. In the first place, this movement began in response to the problem of discrimination against certain communities (*hisabetsu burakumin*) within the sect. Hakamaya sought the cause for this within the doctrine of *hongaku*. In other words, this doctrine accepts present conditions as they are, and from the standpoint of "discrimination, while being discrimination, is permanent and does not pass away," results in the reinforcing and rationalization of the discrimination in the present.

Hakamaya entitled his own book *Criticisms of Hongaku Philosophy*,[6] and hurled criticisms against *hongaku* philosophy head on. Hakamaya's criticisms contain misunderstandings of this doctrine, and therefore I cannot simply affirm his stance. But it is extremely significant in that he links *hongaku* with the ethical problems in contemporary Japan, and arrives at the most foundational question of "What is Buddhism, really?"

Hongaku theory was something that developed during the Japanese Middle Ages, and is therefore thought to be unique to Japan. If that is the case, the lack of ethics that stems from this theory is not part of the essence of Buddhism, but would seem to be a problem peculiar to Japan as a region. However, a similar affirmation of the present can also be seen in Chinese Chan (Zen) Buddhism, so it is not necessarily restricted to Japan. Not only that, Matsumoto Shirō sees the beginnings of this thought in the Indian concept of *Tathāgatagarbha* (see Chapter 7), and thus criticizes even early Buddhist thought.[7]

Therefore, this is not just a regional problem, but perhaps we can say that it is a problem inherent in the essence of the Buddhist religion. So, beyond the borders of Japan, we need to rethink even the things that have come from Indian Buddhism.

6. Hakamaya Noriaki 袴谷憲昭『本覚思想批判』[Criticisms of *hongaku* philosophy] (Japan: Daizō Shuppan, 1989).

7. See Matsumoto Shirō 松本史朗『縁起と空』[Dependent arising and emptiness] (Tokyo: Daizō Shuppan, 1989).

3

The Ethicality of Early Buddhism

If one examined the breadth of Japanese Buddhism, I doubt if one could simply declare that Buddhism is indeed concerned with ethics. At the very least, there is much room for Buddhism to be criticized in that respect. But how is it with Indian Buddhism? The founder of Buddhism was Gautama Siddhārtha of the Śākya clan, who is called Buddha, which means "a person who has attained enlightenment." He is also called Shakuson (in Japanese) or Śākyamuni Buddha, which both mean the revered one from the Śākya clan. The term "early Buddhism" covers the period of Buddha's life until the time when Buddhism separated into various factions. The tradition flowing from early Buddhism until the present form of Buddhism in Sri Lanka and South East Asia (called Theravāda) is frequently said to possess a strongly ethical character. This is one reason why Theravāda Buddhism quickly caught the attention of people in Western Europe.

For example, out of all the Buddhist sutras, one of early Buddhism's sutras, the *Dhammapada*, is the one most translated into various languages and is beloved all over the world. Within its extremely simple verse, words of deep wisdom on human life are written in a way quite easily understood, even if one is not a Buddhist believer:

> Indeed, in this world, if one repays resentments with more resentment, the breath of resentment will never stop. To breathe is to throw away resentment. This is the eternal truth.[8]

8. Nakamura Hajime 中村元, trans.,『真理のことば・感興のことば』[Buddha's words of truth and words of inspiration] (Tokyo: Iwanami Shoten, 1978), verse 4.

If a person does something evil, do not repeat it. Do not take evil things to heart. Letting evil pile up within is suffering. If a person does something good, then you should return it. Take good things to heart. Letting goodness heap up within leads to joy.[9]

All things are frightened into violence; all things are afraid of death. Putting oneself in the other's place, do not kill; do not force another to kill.[10]

Each word brims with truth and has the power to move any human being. It is not just Buddhists who wish to set aside resentment and violence and realize a peaceful and tranquil world. The fundamental teaching of Buddhism is not particularly unique and is almost common sense.

Do not do anything evil, do good things, purify your heart; this is the teaching of all the buddhas.[11]

This is the the *gāthā* on the precepts shared by the seven buddhas, and is taught as the root of all Buddhism. The Chinese translation reads: 諸善奉行、諸悪莫作、自浄其意、是諸仏教.

WHAT IS "EVIL"?

So, when we speak of "good" or "evil," what do these mean? "Evil" is represented by the five sins of Buddhism: killing, stealing, sexual misconduct, false speech, and intoxication. The five precepts of Buddhism warn against these five sins, and are the most fundamental of Buddhist rules.

For something more systematic, we have the "ten evil deeds." People's deeds are divided into three activities: action, speech, and thought. Evil actions consist of killing, stealing, and sexual misconduct; evil

9. Ibid., verses 117–18.
10. Ibid., verse 129.
11. Ibid., verse 182.

speech includes lying, exaggeration, slander, double-tongued speech (words that cause friction among people); evil thoughts are things like attachment, aversion, and ignorance. Of these, the three forms of evil thought are also called the three poisons and are considered the most fundamental causes of suffering. In order to put an end to the ten evil deeds, there are the ten good acts.

Incidentally, why are these considered evil, and the opposite of these considered as good? In this case, the meaning will be somewhat different for priests and nuns who have discarded secular life in order to devote themselves to practice, and for the laity who still continue with their secular lives while believing in Buddha. For the laity, good acts lead to being reborn into good circumstances, such as rebirth in heaven after death. Conversely, evil deeds lead to being reborn into circumstances filled with difficulty—for instance, being reborn in hell. This way of thinking presupposes the idea of transmigration (*saṃsāra*), wherein we are born and reborn in this world. This idea of transmigration is not exclusive to Buddhism, but rather is a common feature in Indian thought. But in Buddhism, living things (excluding plants) are believed to transmigrate across the six realms: the hell realm, the realm of hungry ghosts, of animals, of *asuras*, of humans, and of *devas*. Those who exist in *saṃsāra* are called sentient beings.

As long as we are within *saṃsāra*, no matter how good the circumstances we are born into are, there is still the possibility of falling into bad circumstances. There is no escaping a sense of anxiety. Because of this, we are never free from suffering. This is why the ultimate goal or *telos* of human beings is liberation from the wheel of rebirth—enlightenment, also called *nirvāṇa*. In order to attain enlightenment, one needs to leave secular life, and undergo spiritual practices. For household leavers (monks and nuns), out of the three divisions of the noble eightfold path—ethical conduct (S. *sīla*), concentration (*samādhi*), and wisdom (*prajñā*)—it is the first that is the foundation of spiritual practice. This is what we call "avoiding evil and doing good."

But why are evil deeds the cause of the cycle of rebirth? Because action and speech are the manifestations of mind (J. *i, kokoro*), the deepest roots lie in the worldly desires of the mind. In Buddhism, the state of one's mind is accorded the highest importance. Even the first verse of the *Dhammapada* says that, "Everything is founded upon the mind, is ruled by the mind, and is constructed by the mind." The worldly desires that come from the mind are precisely those that bind people to this world. Worldly desires are none other than the attachment to this world.

The principle of dependent arising (J. *engi*; S. *pratītyasamutpāda*) explains why the cycle of rebirth keeps going. It says that the suffering of old age and death is brought about by the attachment to this world. Even though we know that *saṃsāra* is filled with suffering, we get more and more attached to this world, and so karmic rebirth endlessly repeats itself. In the schema of twelve-fold dependent arising, where this process is detailed, ignorance (S. *avidyā*) is placed at the foundation of the series of causation. There have been many arguments as to how to interpret the idea of ignorance, but it is clearly not just an intellectual ignorance. If that were the case, one would attain liberation merely by knowing this theory. However, even though one may understand this theory perfectly in an intellectual way, one is not necessarily freed from attachment. Ignorance goes beyond intellectual understanding and binds human beings to this world.

Concretely, how then do we free ourselves from ignorance? We need to cast off the various attachments we have to this world and purify our minds. If we purify our minds, it inevitably follows that we also avoid evil in our actions and speech. However, because the laity cannot completely cast off worldly desires, it is impossible for the laity to free themselves from *saṃsāra*. Because of this, emancipation from the wheel of rebirth requires that one leave the householder life and engage in spiritual practices.

In this way, according to the tradition flowing from early Buddhism to schools such as Theravāda, in order to still the workings of worldly desires, it is necessary to discipline everyday life. It is this that forms the ethical character of Buddhism. This is formalized in the noble eightfold path—right view, right intention, right speech, right action, right livelihood, right effort, right mindfulness, and right concentration.

However, seen this way, the ideal life is a purely individual one. In *saṃsāra*, one reaps what one sows, and nobody else is responsible for the result of one's actions except oneself. Avoiding evil and pursuing good are purely at a personal level. In verse 35 of the *Sutta Nipāta*, it is said: "Like the horn of a rhinoceros, one walks alone." This has been the most basic principle since early Buddhism.

THE IDEAL COMMUNITY

Even though the general principle is that one traverses the path alone, in reality, disciples gathered around Śākyamuni and naturally formed a group. This autonomous group was made up of spiritual practitioners who walked together toward the same aim: seeking enlightenment. This group is what we call the *saṅgha* (S. *saṃgha*).

When a group forms, one needs rules. These rules are the precepts. Therefore, while precepts are themselves good acts, they are also rules that maintain the existence of the *saṅgha*. A system of precepts with over 200 clauses developed; and taken together, these are called the *vinaya*. Only those who abide by these are allowed to be members of the *saṅgha*. The monks are called *bhikkhu* (male), and the nuns are called *bhikkhunī* (female), and they form the core of this religious organization.

The *saṅgha* is an equal, democratic organization; one is not allowed to bring one's social class within secular society into the *saṅgha*, and only the number of years since one has entered religious service determines one's position. When the religious organization became big, it split and conducted activities in various places. But ultimately, all the household-leaver practitioners formed an ideal universal *saṅgha*.

However, in actuality, things did not go so smoothly. Inner conflicts and differences of opinion frequently occurred, and the religious organization split into various schools because of that. In any case, what is so interesting is that spiritual practitioners, who aimed for a solitary practice, constructed, for that very purpose, a pure, ideal community, which was otherwise impossible in secular society.

Not only that, but another important point is that such a *saṃgha* community is by no means cut off from secular society. The *saṃgha* is not a self-sufficient, closed organization. In order for ascetics to focus on their practice, they need the support of the laity, for example by giving food when the ascetics go on begging rounds. And by preaching, they earn support for their daily life, thus creating a relationship of mutual dependence. This reciprocal relationship between the religious group of practitioners and the lay believers has transcended history and has continued unbroken, from Śākyamuni's time, all the way up to the societies in present day Southeast Asia.

From the standpoint of Mahāyāna Buddhism, which calls itself the "greater vehicle," the abovementioned (Theravāda) Buddhism is "Hīnayāna Buddhism," a Buddhism that is a "smaller vehicle," wherein one seeks no more than one's own enlightenment. They criticize Theravāda's self-righteous stance, which fails to consider the salvation of others. But despite that criticism, Theravāda did form a definite sense of community, built a stable relationship with the secular society, and maintained ethical norms of conduct. In contrast, Mahāyāna Buddhism, while asserting the need to not merely aim for one's own enlightenment but the salvation of others as well, ended up with the breakdown of ethics. How paradoxical; how ironic. As soon as the problems of the other come into the field, the self-sufficiency of the ethical world collapses, and we are thrust into difficulties that cannot be resolved within the domain of *ningen*.

4

The Bodhisattva Theory of the Other

Early Buddhism focused on the individual unit. Let us consider "not killing," the foundation of the precepts. While killing can only occur if there is an "other" to be killed, *not* killing does not necessarily suppose another party. Of course, if interpreted positively, this precept can mean "valuing life," but it does not necessarily refer to that. The same is the case with not stealing: Stealing requires another party from whom to steal, but a person doing spiritual practices alone, in a mountain, in the middle of nowhere, would have nobody to steal from in the first place. While evil needs an other in order to come about, good does not necessarily require an other.

As I mentioned previously, this is not necessarily a rejection of ethics. Rather, one can argue that it is amongst autonomous individuals who respect each other and live in accordance with the laws that ethics can come to be. Modern social contract theory sees autonomously surviving individuals as coming into a contract in order to coordinate their interests, thus forming a state. A similar line of thought can be seen in early Buddhist scriptures, which are known to be founded on an exceptionally rational view. Early Buddhism aims at a foundation wherein affective attachments cease and a rational way of life can be constructed.

THE PRINCIPLES OF AWAKENING AND COMPASSION

Of course there are also virtues in early Buddhism wherein one actively works for the sake of an other. "Compassion" (*jihi*) is an important virtue, even in early Buddhism. However, it is not quite clear what role it plays in the system of ethics.

When Buddha attained enlightenment, he thought that the people of the world would never understand what he had realized anyway, and he considered simply enjoying this state of bliss until his final days, without bothering to teach it to anyone. But the chief god of Earth, Brahmā, thought that if Buddha dies without teaching what he had finally realized, many suffering people will remain unsaved. And so he implored Buddha to teach, and after three rounds of heartfelt begging, Buddha finally relented and agreed. This is a famous story called "Brahmā's Request" (*bonten kanjō*).

Perhaps we can read this story as a fictional narration of the actual hesitation and indecision Buddha felt within, and the process of overcoming that and resolving to teach. If so, quibbling about what would have happened if Brahmā had not implored Buddha might seem to be splitting hairs. However, looking at it from this story, if Brahmā had not done so, then we might not have the Buddha's expounding of the dharma at all. This shows us that "one must teach for the sake of people" is *not* central to Buddha's realization. This is because, if the idea that "this insight must be shared to all" had been present within the core of the truth he realized, there would have been no room for hesitation to occur at all.

Preaching the teachings to people and saving them from suffering was Buddha's highest act of compassion, but surprisingly, this was not necessarily the core of the truth he realized. Even if he had quietly passed away, completely alone and secluded, this would not have gone against the essence of his enlightenment. Nevertheless, Buddha preached the dharma. But if so, then that would be something that emanates from a separate principle, outside the truth he had realized. That means that the principle of compassion is located separately from the principle of enlightenment.

However, looking at the missionary work of Buddha during the latter part of his life, one must admit that there was nothing trifling about his acts of compassion—it was tied to Buddha's very own spiritual core. Although it may not be part of the principle of enlightenment, if one considers the difficulties he had to overcome in order to preach, his compassion becomes even more worthy of respect. Why would anyone be surprised by the practice of something already contained within the principle of enlightenment? But if one puts into practice something not even contained within principles, it becomes an act without compensation, a pure act based on none other than the love for others.

In actuality, as Buddha had already attained enlightenment, whether or not he taught would have made no difference to his essence as Buddha. Rather, by teaching, he involved himself with others, and the trouble and complications that come with that.

In this way, there are two distinct streams in the principles of early Buddhism. First is what is contained in Buddha's enlightenment, which was eventually systematized in the four noble truths and the noble eightfold path. Second is that which motivated his missionary activities in the latter part of his life—the principle of compassion without recompense, which is not in itself included in enlightenment. This did not end with Buddha; the disciples who received his teaching went on to preach passionately in various places. Thanks to this, Buddhism, which was of course transmitted throughout India, was brought to Ceylon (Sri Lanka), and eventually to Southeast Asia, thus building the strong tradition of Theravāda Buddhism.

COMPASSION NEEDS AN "OTHER"

While this may be quite clear from our previous considerations, compassion necessarily requires the other as the opposite party to whom one extends compassion. This is clear if we compare compassion to the aforementioned precepts on not killing and not stealing. These precepts can function even without any others. Rather, it is the reverse—killing and stealing—that need an other in order to be possible. Rather than not killing or not stealing, compassion can be put in the same category as killing and stealing, as it presupposes an other.

This argument might smack of sophistry, but it is the existence of the other that introduces all this complexity to the problems at hand. For Buddha, taken as an ideal person, compassion that is genuinely without recompense might be possible. However, if one has the slightest taint of worldly desires remaining, then there goes the guarantee of maintaining the purity of non-compensation in human relations. Even though one may have peace of mind when alone, when human relations come into the picture—jealousy and competition, love and hate—a slew of complicated emotions come with it.

It is known that while Buddha was alive, there were cases of libel and conflict within the sangha. Also, it is said that the reason why the precepts were put into place one by one was because of the various problems in the sangha. And worse, when Buddha passed away, things took a turn for the worse—there were various schisms and disagreements in the interpretation of the teachings. Building ideal human relations is by no means easy.

The monk Devadatta is famous for rebelling against the Buddha. But even if he actually had advocated a more ascetic view of practice, it is doubtful that he was as terrible as he was made to seem. When a particular group is formed, it is often the case (and unsurprisingly) that all manners of evils are forced upon heretics like him, as one would to a scapegoat.

Another example is the monk Mahādeva, who is seen as the cause of the first schism, and who taught five heresies. Amongst those heresies are some very graphic ideas, for instance that even an *arhat* has wet dreams. Of course, wet dreams do not need an other. But my point is that these problems occur largely because of the human relationships within a group. The theory of early Buddhism is able to thoroughly adhere to the rationality of fundamental truth only by excluding the above-mentioned irrational elements that arise within relationships with others.

THE BURDEN OF THE "OTHER"

The distinctness of Mahāyāna Buddhism from early Buddhism is that the former tries to incorporate the relationship with the other into its fundamental principles. The Mahāyāna spirit is embodied in the figure of the bodhisattva, who aims at simultaneously realizing both his or her own spiritual salvation and that of others. While self-benefit (in the spiritual sense) can be carried out without an other, benefitting others is impossible without the other. In this way, Mahāyāna incorporates the existence of others into its core principles.

Just because people cannot live without others, it does not follow that one naturally needs to include others *in principle*. It is possible, as in the case of early Buddhism, to not include them. However, as soon as one incorporates relationships with others, things get complicated. The other is not indifferent to the I, nor does the other leave the I be. Feelings irreducible to the rational, like fond attachment or hatred, start to stir up. Problems come up even amongst mutually autonomous religious practitioners. When one relates with ordinary people or people outside one's religion, there is no way things will pass quietly.

When one makes the relationship with others a matter of principle, one presupposes that these circumstances will inevitably arise. Perhaps in some cases, these can even lead to conflict and violence. Issues like these are actually taken up in Mahāyāna scriptures. In this way, Mahāyāna Buddhism bears insoluble and burdensome issues that would otherwise be unthinkable in the community of early Buddhism, taken as a collection of isolated individuals. Ethics does not become clearer when we bear the other in mind. To the contrary, the laws of ethics become muddled and are slowly eroded. The other is a strange thing that strays beyond the rules of *ningen*.

In the face of the complex problems that arise because of the incorporation of the other into its core principles, rather than drowning in these issues, Mahāyāna Buddhism constructed additional principles to resist such a defeat and realize the ideal. One example is the six perfections, constructed as the ethics of bodhisattvas, which charge each person with an infinite demand. "Perfection" (S. *pāramitā*) means "completion," and includes the virtues of generosity, moral discipline, forbearance, effort, concentration, and wisdom. These virtues are not carried out half-heartedly, but ought to be thoroughly pursued. In this sense, it differs from the thinking of early Buddhism, which emphasizes moderation and avoids extremes.

Another example is the attempt to thoroughly realize "emptiness" (J. *kū*; S. *śūnyatā*) in order to resist attachment. While emptiness is the theoretical core of Mahāyāna Buddhism, in praxis it means distancing oneself from one's attachments, and seeking a state of freedom where one is unimpeded.

However, does the construction of principles like these really prevent Buddhism from sinking into the proverbial quicksand? Does it not accomplish the reverse, making problems even more complicated? Thoroughly realizing "perfections" is by no means an easy task. And freedom without attachments—would this not just fall into an expedient moral lawlessness? In this way, Mahāyāna Buddhism ended up shouldering many complex issues that were absent in early Buddhism.

5

From Ethics to Trans-Ethics

The root of Mahāyāna Buddhism is the bodhisattva spirit, which aims for the salvation of others and not merely one's own salvation. This seems like such a wonderful thing, but in reality it actually jeopardizes ethics. But precisely for this reason, the other becomes all the more prominent. I would like to look at this concretely from a more historical perspective.

The Japanese transliteration of bodhisattva is *bosatsu*. *Bodhi* means enlightenment, and *sattva* are living beings or sentient beings—those, including humans, who travel about the six realms. Those two words tied together make bodhisattva, and in the simplest terms, it is understood to mean a living being who seeks enlightenment. It is not a concept invented along with Mahāyāna Buddhism, but one that had been established before, and is a word that points to Buddha's state of being before he attained enlightenment.

In accordance with the idea of *saṃsāra*, Buddha did not just attain enlightenment through practice within one lifetime. To attain the ultimate truth, he must have undergone an infinitely long time of practice throughout repeated cycles of rebirth. The Jātaka tales (birth stories) come from such a premise. It is a literary genre that tells of the good deeds of Buddha in his previous lives.

According to the research of specialists, the beginnings of the Jātaka tales and the process of its connecting to the idea of bodhisattvas are a bit complicated, but I will not go into that now. Anyhow, these kinds of tales can be seen in carvings found in Buddhist stupas like Bharhut, and these carvings have been around since 2 BCE.

Aside from being written in the *Tipiṭaka* in Pali, there are many Chinese translations, and these tales considerably influenced Japanese narrative literature. Let us look at some well-known tales.

"The Tale of the Rabbit" reads as follows:

> There was once a rabbit, a monkey, an otter, and a fox, who all lived in the mountains together, listening to a hermit preach. The hermit wanted to move to a place where there was more food, and so in order to get the hermit to stay, these four animals foraged food for him. The monkey, otter, and fox all brought food for the hermit, but the rabbit was not able to find any. So, the rabbit tried to offer his own body, and jumped into the fire. The fire was put out and the rabbit was saved. And the hermit stayed and lived together with the animals.[12] (A sequel exists, wherein by the power of the deity Śakra Devānām-Indra, the image of the rabbit is now enshrined permanently on the moon.)

Another story is entitled "The Tale of King Shibi":

> There once was a great king named Shibi. One day, in order to test the king, the deity Śakra Devānām-Indra and his follower Viśvakarman disguised themselves as a falcon and a dove. The falcon chased the dove and the dove sought refuge with the king. In order to save the dove, the king offered to give the falcon a piece of his flesh from his own body equivalent to the weight of the dove. Strangely, however much of the king's flesh was sliced and weighed in the scale, the body of the dove was still heavier, so the king offered his whole body to the falcon. At this point, the falcon and the dove appeared in their true forms and praised the virtue of the king.[13]

These are both stories of sacrificing one's own body, and the story of King Shibi can famously be seen even in cave paintings in Central Asia. Similarly, the story of "The Hungry Tigress,"[14] wherein Buddha,

---

12. See 『六度集経』 [Sutra on the collection of the six destinies], Book 3.
13. See 『大智度論』 [*Mahāprajñāpāramitā-śāstra*], Book 25.
14. See 『金光明経』 [The golden light sutra].

in a previous incarnation, sacrifices his body to feed a starving tigress, is drawn on the Tamamushi Shrine in Hōryū-ji.

As I mentioned in the previous chapter, we can see the six perfections as examples of the virtues of a bodhisattva; however, the practice of these virtues must be carried out thoroughly, to their extreme limit. Sacrificing one's body in order to aid another is equivalent to the *pāramitā* of generosity; however, when one sacrifices one's own body, nothing more can be given. This is definitely not something anyone can easily do. Precisely because of this, the previous incarnations of Buddha gain special significance. And so originally, "bodhisattva" referred to the previous incarnations of Buddha, rather than something achievable by ordinary people.

MULTIPLE BUDDHAS

However, circumstances are different when we consider Mahāyāna Buddhism. One major unique characteristic of Mahāyāna Buddhism is that it recognizes many buddhas, rather than merely one person as Buddha.

Originally, the general idea was that in one era, there can only be one Buddha, and therefore, the existence of buddhas in the present world other than the historical Śākyamuni Buddha was not recognized. However, there is a theory that became prevalent early on called *Kako shichibutsu*, according to which seven buddhas appeared in the past, and Śākyamuni is the seventh. In addition, people began believing from early on that Maitreya would come in the future as the eighth Buddha. However, because buddhas outside of Śākyamuni cannot exist in the present world, no matter how hard an ordinary person may try, his or her enlightenment would be different from that of Buddha, and he or she could not become a buddha.

Mahāyāna Buddhism did away with this limitation. One way of resolving it was by recognizing the existence of other worlds in the present. In this world, sure, there is only one Buddha. However, what if there were other worlds outside of this one? If there are other worlds, then certainly, buddhas other than Śākyamuni can exist.

If there are *countless* worlds, then countless buddhas are also possible. As an example, Akṣobhya is the Buddha in the realm of profound joy to the East. Amitābha is the Buddha in the Western paradise. It is only by exercising a lot of creativity that an idea like this can be conceived.

The process of the spiritual practice of bodhisattvas was gradually formalized. As typically exemplified by Amitābha, in a previous life, one first gives rise to the resolve to attain enlightenment and takes an oath in front of Buddha. When this is recognized by Buddha, he gives an assurance (S. *vyākaraṇa*) that one will become a buddha in the future. After a long period of practice, one realizes this oath and becomes a buddha.

At the same time, the bodhisattva's ideal form is also described in concrete terms. A typical example is the bodhisattva Kannon (Avalokiteśvara). Kannon is said to have thirty-three selves, he has various avatars in order to bring salvation to living things. Kannon represents the altruistic nature of Mahāyāna Buddhism. Aside from Kannon, we also have bodhisattvas like Mañjuśrī and Samantabhadra, who have various unique characteristics.

Toward the Buddha as Savior

Incidentally, recognizing the existence of countless buddhas opened up two contradictory possibilities. First, if countless buddhas are possible, then provided one practices relentlessly, anyone can become a buddha. Here, the focus shifts to practice that is based on the six perfections, which the Buddha had previously performed. This is certainly a difficult path, but since the Jātaka tales point out a model for bodhisattva practice, if one could overcome these difficulties, anyone could follow this model and become a buddha. Speaking from that point of view, the practice that appears in the Jātaka tales is both the way that my savior Buddha practiced, and the way I ought to practice if I myself am to be a bodhisattva.

However, while this is ideal, it is so extreme that it is virtually impossible to abide by in everyday life. Not just anyone can go to the extreme of sacrificing one's own body in an act of total generosity. Also, as the formula goes, it takes three *asaṃkhyeya kalpas* to complete the bodhisattva's practice in order to become a buddha. Both *asaṃkhyeya* (10 to the 56th or 64th powers) and *kalpa* (eon) are numerical units, but they approach infinity, so in other words, infinite practice is necessary. To hear this is overwhelming, and it seems completely out of this world.

Let us consider the second possibility. Recognizing the existence of countless buddhas made the Buddha seem more superhuman, and gave rise to the tendency to see buddhas as saviors. While the idea of the superhuman-ness of Buddha was growing even before the rise of Mahāyāna Buddhism, it took a step further in this direction, with the remains of Buddha being enshrined in pagodas (stupas) and Buddha becoming the object of worship.

Originally, in Buddhism, one reaps what one sows; one is responsible for the consequences of one's own actions. For that reason, the idea of being saved by an other is, at the very least, not part of the essence of Buddhism. However, with the rise of the abovementioned developments, the idea of salvation took to the fore. Buddha is a savior, and I am one of the sentient beings to be saved by this Buddha. If this is the case, then that overwhelmingly long period of practice is no longer necessary.

THE OTHER CALLED BUDDHA

Let us look at this from the point of view of ethics. The six perfections are certainly ethical virtues, and it would be absolutely wonderful if these could be put into practice. However, if one undertook this by oneself, there is no way it would be easy. In everyday life, we cannot throw down our lives as an offering. This idea itself already goes beyond the level of the ethics of *ningen*.

Because the requirements are too demanding, they become futile and impossible to fulfill, and so in a backlash of sorts, one ends up depending on salvation from Buddha instead. This is how the first possibility leads to the second. However, if it is Buddha who is the one who extends salvation to others, then I will be exempted from responsibility. The six perfections then fail to fulfill their ethical role—a complete reversal from an impossibly heavy ethical responsibility to an entrusting to Buddha (who is other to me), which thus releases oneself from this responsibility. This is what the True Pure Land thinker Kiyozawa Manshi termed as the conversion from infinite responsibility to irresponsibility (see Chapter 13).

Now, we have a new problem of the other: How do I relate with the Buddha (the other) who saves me? The Buddha is yet another other who cannot fully be reduced to the orders of the ethical. With the arrival of the Buddha, an entirely unknowable, gigantic other, we are presented with a new aspect to the problem of relating with others. In Chapter 15, I would like to think about the Buddha as an other by taking *The Lotus Sutra* as an example.

Well then, is the first path completely impossible? Here, too, people devised schemes in order to figure out easier ways to achieve enlightenment. For example, in Zen, we have the idea of sudden enlightenment, wherein enlightenment can be achieved in the present life. If so, there is no need for that overwhelming idea of unending practice. Enlightenment thus becomes an achievable thing; it can be achieved through one's own powers, without relying on others. Taken to an extreme, this leads to the doctrine of *hongaku*, but if so, the practices by which we relate to others as bodhisattvas become lax.

Thus, in both the first and second path, the original bodhisattva spirit, which includes a movement towards the other, becomes weaker. In its place, as in the case of the second path, a new interpersonal problem of how to face the Buddha directly as the other emerges. In either case, the ethics of *ningen*, which was the order of things in early Buddhism, can no longer hold true. And from the place of the impossibility of that ethics, we need the religiosity of the trans-ethical.

6

The Ambiguity of the Principle of Emptiness

It is said that the foundational idea of Mahāyāna Buddhism is "emptiness." The line from the *Heart Sutra*, "Form as it is, is emptiness, emptiness as it is, is form," is probably the most familiar to Japanese people. But what does "emptiness" mean? This discussion might get a bit abstract, I apologize in advance.

"Emptiness" is said to mean "nonsubstantiality." In other words, there is no existence in this world that exists in itself and of itself, eternally and without change. This concept did not just suddenly crop up in Mahāyāna Buddhism. It originally came from the early Buddhist principles of no-self (S. *anātman*) and dependent origination (S. *pratītyasamutpāda*, alternatively translated as [inter/co-]dependent [co-]arising/origination).

Everything that exists in this world comes about because of dependent origination. That means that their existence inevitably has a cause, and nothing can exist alone and autonomously. All existence in this world is bound by relationships of cause and effect. Because of this, if circumstances change, then existences change, and thus no existence is perpetual or immutable. That is what is called "no-self." Therefore, dependent origination and no-self are equivalent, and "emptiness" is a restatement of that as well.

However, as a new word, emptiness must have some distinct part from dependent origination and no-self. Now what would that be? The word "emptiness" originally meant that something was lacking, and, to that extent, means a particular state of lacking something. However, Mahāyāna Buddhism often uses it to concisely express the structure of the world as a whole. It is well-known that meditation, also known as *samādhi*, played an important role in the formation of Mahāyāna Buddhism. Emptiness is something that one arrives at all at once in that *samādhi*. On that point, dependent origination and no self merely express the analytic and rational understanding of individual phenomena, whereas emptiness is an immediate, embodied realization.

However, emptiness is theoretically elucidated in philosophical debates, and Mahāyāna Buddhism does articulate the stages leading up to the attainment of enlightenment. The *Flower Garland Sutra* (S. *Avataṃsaka sūtra*) discusses these stages, called the *daśabhūmi*. Also, we have the story about the wealthy boy who goes on a pilgrimage in order to find a master who can guide him on the way. In these, we see that it takes an enormous amount of effort to attain enlightenment. Similarly, in the *prajñā* (wisdom) literature, we have the story of the spiritual quest of the bodhisattva Sadāprarudita. This complex ascent to enlightenment is discussed not only in Tibetan Buddhism but in the Tientai and Huayen schools in Chinese Buddhism.

However, this austere developmental theory is often made vague. In China's Chan Buddhism we have the idea of sudden enlightenment, and in Japan's Esoteric Buddhism we have the idea of attaining Buddhahood in this body / life (*sokushin jōbutsu*). There was a fondness for conceptions of attaining enlightenment without passing through stages, and the developmental approach was slowly forgotten. With this, philosophies wherein one could instantly attain the ultimate truth of emptiness began to spread, often in an irresponsible and lackadaisical form.

THE DOUBLE ENTENDRE OF EMPTINESS

In practice, emptiness links up with the notion of non-attachment. If all existence in this world is *empty*, then all things are subject to change, and it is therefore meaningless to cling to them. If one is not caught up with anything, then one can move with total freedom. Through an immediate and embodied realization of emptiness, one arrives at a great sense of freedom. But can it not be said that because one is empty and unattached, one can flippantly change one's opinion depending on the circumstances? In times of war, one can support war, and in times of peace, one can preach pacifism—is this not non-attachment, the practice of emptiness? Are we really okay with this? This is also connected with the collapse of ethics in Mahāyāna Buddhism.

This sort of loose interpretation is particularly conspicuous in Japanese Buddhism, but its roots can be found in the philosophy of emptiness itself. Previously, I mentioned the line from the *Heart Sūtra* which goes, "Form, as it is, is emptiness; Emptiness, as it is, is form." The phrase "as it is, is" (*soku*) is the culprit here. "Form" is the first of the five bundles (S. *skandha*, the others are feeling, perception, mental formations, and consciousness), and it refers to material existence. But this form exists as empty ("Form, as it is, is emptiness") and conversely, emptiness does not exist abstractly, separate from the concrete *topos* of form ("Emptiness, as it is, is form").

However, this is usually understood to mean that the concrete phenomenal forms (the world of the unenlightened) are, as they are, essentially identical with absolute emptiness (the world of enlightenment). If these two are seen as identical then the world of delusion is at once the world of wisdom and there is no need to alter the world of the unenlightened. Japanese *hongaku* philosophy developed that tendency to an extreme. We have sayings like, "Worldly desires, as they are, are enlightenment," "Good and evil are two faces of the same coin,"[15] which are understood as meaning that worldly desires and evil are fine as they are. Ethics thus becomes quite impossible.

When one says "emptiness," it includes a negative nuance. But it is also spoken of positively—"the ultimate nature of things" (J. *shinnyo*,

---

15. 煩惱即菩提, 善惡不二.

S. *tathatā*) or "the true state of affairs." This entire world is the world of the Buddha. With this, the tendency to simply affirm the phenomenal world just the way it is grows stronger. Because the little flowers that grow by the roadside and insects are all living within the world of the Buddha, then no existence is without worth. Therefore, one must value all life, no matter how lowly. I myself came by this teaching when I was young and despairing of my own life, and I cannot express just how much peace this has brought me.

That being said, there is another side to this story. If the above held true, because everything occurred in the world of the Buddha, then no matter how much evil I wrought, , it would be quite alright. It is like the Monkey King (Sun Wukong) in the palm of Buddha's hand—no matter where he goes, or what he does, he cannot leap out beyond the world of the Buddha.

Taking a hint from the *Vimalakīrti Sutra*

Let us look at the ambiguity of emptiness a bit more concretely, making use of the scripture called the *Vimalakīrti Sutra*. This sutra takes Vimalakīrti, a lay Buddhist, as its protagonist. It is a rather thrilling story in which he criticizes the disciples of the Buddha (who were monks, rather than laypersons) from a Mahāyāna standpoint. It was translated into Chinese by Kumārajīva (344–413 CE, according to some theories 350–409), who also translated the *Lotus Sutra*. It was very much beloved by Chinese intellectuals, who themselves stressed lay Buddhism. Vimalakīrti was considered to be the very ideal of lay Buddhists.

In the *Vimalakīrti Sutra*, Buddha's disciples and other bodhisattvas, led by the bodhisattva Mañjuśrī, pay a visit to Vimalakīrti, who lay ill. The story is composed of the various questions and answers that occurred in this visit. Vimalakīrti's illness itself was actually a provisional manifestation in order to save sentient beings. "Because all sentient beings are ill, I am ill." These oft-quoted words express the ideal spirit of the bodhisattva.

Vimalakīrti's room is "empty" in the literal sense. He does not even have attendants. He says, "All the demons and the heretics are my attendants. Why, you ask? While all demons enjoy life and death, a bodhisattva does not dispose of life and death. Heretics enjoy all sorts of opinions, but a bodhisattva does not part from these opinions." Demons, heretics, and bodhisattvas are all living within the circle of life and death. However, while demons and heretics are attached to life and death, various opinions, and the like, bodhisattvas neither cast these away nor cling to them. That is the difference between them.

Another way of expressing it is by saying, "Although one preaches that this body is impermanent, one does not preach parting from this body. Although one preaches that this body is suffering, one does not preach the desire for *nirvāṇa*." The suffering of life and death and the tranquility of *nirvāṇa* are not separate. To begin with, it is an error to set up *saṃsāra* and *nirvāṇa* as dualities. Both are inseparable—that is the meaning of emptiness.

One of the highlights of the *Vimalakīrti Sutra* is the chapter "The Dharma Gate of Nonduality." Here, we see different conflicting expressions (supposedly said by different bodhisattvas), and it is said that these dualities are originally "not two." For instance, arising and perishing, good and not good (evil), sin and blessedness, the state of being defiled by passions and the state of being free from them,[16] the lay world and the monastic world, *saṃsāra* and *nirvāṇa*—these conflicting parts are not two, not separate from each other.

"Not two" means the transcending of the conflict of two concepts, thus arriving at a higher stage. However, one may argue that since two conflicting concepts are identical anyway, then good and evil are identical, the state of having desires and not having desires are identical, and thus *saṃsāra*, as it is, is *nirvāṇa*. If one interprets it this way, then

16. 有漏, 無漏.

the status quo is affirmed as it is, and it becomes unnecessary to introduce any changes. This would end up maintaining the status quo, and all further development would cease.

MAHĀYĀNA BUDDHISM AND ETHICS

Above, we considered two fundamental principles of Mahāyāna Buddhism—bodhisattvas and emptiness—and I think one can sense the difficult conundrums that these would bring into ethics.

First, Mahāyāna Buddhism certainly takes up the lofty ideal of saving sentient beings. It preaches the six perfections, and sometimes one is even required to cast away one's own life for the sake of generosity. Also, in order to save sentient beings, one manifests illness in one's own body. Well, that is splendid, but in the first place, is this sort of high-flying salvific activity even within the reach of us ordinary, foolish people?

However, we who are saved ought to be no different from the buddhas and bodhisattvas who save us. Here lies the fundamental difference between Mahāyāna and Christianity. If this is the case, then how are we to bridge the gap between the world of imperfect fools and the lofty, ideal world of buddhas and bodhisattvas? For this, the dead (the deceased), as "others," who function as intermediaries, come into question. I will take this up in Part III of this book.

Second, the principles of Mahāyāna Buddhism problematize this world as a whole. It teaches that we should "save all sentient beings," that this whole world is "empty," "the true suchness," or "the true state of affairs." However, when one takes issue with the whole world in this way, things get blown up disproportionately and one never gets to more concrete forms of ethics. This spells trouble for ethics. In such a setup, all evils are absorbed within the world of the Buddha and are accepted. But this collapse of ethics can also open the way up to trans-ethics.

However, in this case, when one enlarges the problem all too suddenly, there is a danger of ignoring issues that are closer at hand. For example, in the "real world," one would be much more concerned about one's own children rather than a war waged in a distant land. Of course, if one says that this is a form of attachment, and Buddhism is supposed to go beyond that, then that puts an end to the discussion. But is it not more realistic to rethink things from the standpoint of our *inability* to transcend such attachments?

Given that, it would be a mistake to think that we are moving from the world of the ethics of *ningen* to some remote world of the trans-ethical. Even trans-ethics is not removed from the everyday world. Let us take a good look at the everyday world—the world where even though one does not want to be attached to things, one gets attached anyway. Here, though one may try to be ethical, one cannot but notice the "I" that fails at this. The everyday itself is not closed as merely the domain of *ningen*, but rather contains even the trans-ethical that goes beyond *ningen*. Even while speaking of emptiness or not-two-ness, we must take our point of departure from a reconsideration and rethinking of our everyday existence.

7

Can Anyone Become a Buddha?

There is another thing we have to consider with Mahāyāna Buddhism: the philosophy of *Tathāgatagarbha* (J. *Nyoraizō*) or Buddha-nature. Unlike the principles of bodhisattvas and emptiness, this philosophy was not present from the beginnings of Mahāyāna Buddhism, and is thus not accepted by the orthodox schools of Tibet. (Therefore it is not universally present in Mahāyāna Buddhism.) But nevertheless, it had a considerable impact on East Asian Buddhism. Given that, I would like to take it up here, separately from the ideas of bodhisattvas and emptiness.

I will only speak briefly about the birth and theoretical positioning of the philosophy of *Tathāgatagarbha* / Buddha-nature. To put it succinctly, Buddha-nature refers to the possibility or potential to become a buddha. (From this point on, as I will be focusing on East Asian Buddhism, when I write "Buddha," I mean *Hotoke* or *Fo* as it is called in Japanese and Chinese.) The principle of *Tathāgatagarbha* / Buddha-nature is that anyone can become a buddha—that is, everyone has the true nature of being a buddha. There is a slight difference in nuance between *Tathāgatagarbha* and Buddha-nature, but we can take them to mean the same. In East Asia, the line "All sentient beings have the Buddha-nature"[17] from the *Nirvāṇa sūtra* is quite well known. *Tathāgatagarbha* philosophy also spread through the text *Awakening of Faith in Mahāyāna*.

17. 一切衆生に悉く仏性あり.

The philosophy of the bodhisattva in Mahāyāna refutes the tendency to see buddhas as existences disconnected from us ordinary folk. It recognizes that anyone can build up spiritual practice as a bodhisattva and eventually become a buddha. In the concept of *Tathāgatagarbha* / Buddha-nature, this principle becomes even more immanent. Even without constructing such a principle, and even from the principles of Mahāyāna Buddhism, one could already become a buddha so long as one accumulates practice as a bodhisattva. But the theories of *Tathāgatagarbha* / Buddha-nature recognize this anew as an internal, immanent principle.

What changes with the construction of this principle? To put it simply, becoming a buddha (*jōbutsu*) becomes very close at hand. The practices of a bodhisattva supposedly take three *asaṃkhyeya kalpas*, which is an almost infinitely long amount of time. It is almost dizzying just to think of it. In that span, who knows what sort of suffering one might undergo—perhaps one might quit in frustration. So it is very uncertain. But if the true nature of Buddhahood is immanent within each one of us, then things get much easier. Even if one might be set back, it is not like one will lose one's true nature—a comforting idea.

According to the theory of *Tathāgatagarbha* / Buddha-nature, the mind (*kokoro*) is originally pure, and is merely concealed by worldly desires. Thus, if we wipe away the clouding of desire, this pure and true nature will begin to show itself. One is not acquiring some new capacity that one does not presently have; rather, one only needs to manifest the true nature of Buddhahood as a reality. It is based on this optimistic view. However, one might wonder if it might be too optimistic.

THE PRACTICALITY OF THE THEORY OF THE FIVE SEPARATE NATURES

The theory that all have the Buddha-nature is opposed to the Mind-Only Hossō school's theory of the five separate natures. There was a big debate between these two camps in both China and

Japan. The latter theory argues that not all people have the possibility of becoming buddhas, and that this future potential is predetermined. The five natures are as follows:

> *Shōmon teisei*: those who have the true nature of the Hīnayāna *śrāvaka* (those who attain enlightenment due to Buddha's teachings).
>
> *Engaku teisei*: those who have the true nature of the Hīnayāna *pratyekabuddha* (one who attains enlightenment on his own by chancing upon the truth).
>
> *Bosatsu teisei*: those who have the true nature of becoming a Mahāyāna bodhisattva, and can eventually become a buddha.
>
> *Futeisei*: those who can become either of the three.
>
> And last, *mushō*: those who do not have any of these potentials.

So we have the five *teisei* (determined natures) above. It is a rather unsparing sort of theory, particularly for the *mushō* who are abandoned as having no future potential at all.

With the construction of this determinism, no matter how much one practices, all may come to naught. In this case, it seems pointless to bother trying. If one's potential is predetermined, it may seem like it makes no difference whether or not one preaches. However, nobody knows which of the five natures a person possesses, so we have no choice but to believe in the chance that we might have the potential to become buddhas, and strive. Also, there are some people who are "indeterminate," and it is therefore necessary to steer them toward the path of the bodhisattva.

Therefore, the determinism of the five separate natures does not do away with practice. But rather, it calls for the practices of bodhisattvas even more than the theory of universal Buddha-nature. In Japan, the Hossō school flourished in the late Nara period (710–794) and the early Heian period (794–1185), and we had socially involved practitioners like Gyōki (668–749), who worked so hard for the sake of others that he was called "the bodhisattva Gyōki."

Another person from the Hossō school who was called a bodhi-sattva was Tokuitsu. He preached primarily in the Aizu region. He also got into a fierce debate with Saichō (767–822), who believed in the theory that all have Buddha-nature. He went on to critique Kūkai's Shingon esoteric Buddhism and wrote *Pending Words on the Shingon School*. In this book, he is known for having criticized the esoteric idea of attaining Buddhahood in this body as lacking in compassion. One could get so caught up in seeking to become a buddha oneself that one neglects to save others.

From the perspective of attaining Buddha in this body, the strategy is to become a buddha as quickly as possible, then save people using the power of Buddha. But from the standpoint of the Hossō school, becoming a buddha is a matter for the future. Instead, this school emphasizes committing oneself to the practice of saving sentient beings as a bodhisattva. To put it succinctly, theories of becoming Buddha, including the theory of becoming Buddha in this body, that take the Buddha-nature theory as a point of departure, put off the praxis of benefitting others to until after one attains Buddhahood. In contrast, the Hossō school takes such praxis as an urgent concern to be engaged as soon as possible. Considering this, the Hossō school's approach does not immediately go to the trans-ethical, but tries to bring the standpoint of ethics to life.

With the coming of the Kamakura period (1185–1333), the Hossō school no longer strictly adhered to the theory of the separation of the five natures. But despite that, people like Eison (1201–1290), who followed Hossō theories, are well known for having worked hard at saving others—in contrast to "new Buddhism" and their tendency to make light of social praxis. If we go by Shinran (1173–1262), acts of benefitting others come about in *gensō* (the state of returning from the world of enlightenment to this world). In contrast, the tradition of Hossō emphasizes subjective praxis so much as to see it as necessary even in *ōsō* (the stage of practicing for the sake of attaining enlightenment). Against the view that waits to attain enlightenment—where one acquires the Buddha's omnipotence and so can save others unhindered—practicing as a bodhisattva requires subjective effort that is founded on self-responsibility.

THE EQUALITY OF BUDDHA-NATURE CONCEALS ACTUAL INEQUALITY

This kind of theory of five separate natures did not become very influential in East Asia, and the theory of universal Buddha-nature became a presupposition for almost all forms of Buddhism. That anyone has the true nature of Buddhahood means that, as far as religious ability is concerned, we all have the same capabilities. No matter how we may differ in terms of race, ethnic group, gender, economic class, social position, academic ability, intelligence, etc.—in terms of religious ability, we are all absolutely the same. It is certainly an astounding philosophy of equality.

Although in reality, some people are further along the way to the ideal state of enlightenment and others lag behind, this is no more than a difference in degree. When it comes to absolute capacity, good people and absolutely wretched people are not different in the least. In Buddha-nature, we are all the same, and there is no distinction between the great and the small. Incidentally, the same equality can be found in Hōnen's Pure Land school, in relation to the ability to ascend to the pure land.

However, we need to exercise caution here: Equality in Buddha-nature does not in any way oppose inequalities in reality. Quite the opposite, it has considerable potential to be used as a theory that covers up the inequalities of actual life. "Since in the end, all of us will attain Buddhahood, then do put up with the inequalities of the present life." Such a logic comes about quite easily. History proves that Buddhism does not level the inequalities in the world, but rather, was more often used as a theory to calcify and reinforce inequalities.

Also, it is not just humans who possess the Buddha-nature. When one says "all sentient beings," it points to all the existents that transmigrate across the six realms. That means that hungry ghosts, animals, and beings in hell all equally possess the Buddha-nature. In comparison with Christianity, one distinct feature of Buddhism is the belief that even though you might fall into hell, the possibility of salvation is still open to you. In East Asia, there are ideas like "insentient beings have Buddha-nature" or "grasses and trees attain enlightenment,"[18] which show the general view wherein plants and even inorganic things are recognized as having Buddha-nature. It is certainly a wonderful thing that even a single flower by the roadside will become a buddha. This philosophy influenced Japanese art and entertainment culture quite considerably.

However, what does it really mean for grasses and trees to attain Buddhahood? No amount of mental gymnastics can make sense of this. The Japanese doctrine of *hongaku* states that in nature, the process of budding, flowering, and wilting of plants is itself the manifestation of becoming Buddha. This is a very interesting idea from the point of view of the world of arts. But from the point of view of religious practice, this is problematic—it tends to fall into an "as-it-ism" that has no need for praxis. And, seen ethically, it can never give rise to a concrete theory of praxis.

Dōgen re-read "all beings have Buddha-nature" as "all beings *are* Buddha-nature."[19] Not only that, in this case, he sees Buddha-nature not as a mere possibility but as in itself the realized form of Buddha's enlightenment. In seeing the phenomena of this world as in themselves the world of the Buddha, it is similar to the as-it-ism of *hongaku* theory. However, Dōgen differs from that theory in that his view is only possible *within* the process of praxis. However, although Dōgen was

18. 無情仏性; 草木成仏.
19. 悉有仏性; 悉有は仏性なり.

an incredibly ethically-minded Buddhist, this idea did not develop to the extent of ethical usefulness.

Above, we have seen that while the theory of Buddha-nature played a large role in the development of East Asian Buddhism, it has a tendency to be overly optimistic, and it can be very dangerous to brandish it about naively. The Critical Buddhism movement that recently arose directed its critique primarily toward the philosophy of *Tathāgatagarbha* / Buddha-nature.

There is a famous kōan called "Jōshū's *Mu*." When the high priest Jōshū was asked, "Does the dog have Buddha-nature?" he answered, "*Mu*" (no). This *mu* is a very tricky idea in the Zen world, and in response to the question of Buddha-nature's existence or non-existence, it denies the simplistic idea that Buddha-nature exists. This throws the problem back to the starting line. It warns us against naively relying on such a theory of Buddha-nature.

Is it really so that everyone has Buddha-nature? Did Hitler have it? Perhaps it is not a simple matter as merely chiming, "yes."

8

Is Socially Engaged Buddhism
Even Possible?

Up to this point, we have historically examined the foundational concepts of Buddhism and considered parts that might be problematic. When thinking about Mahāyāna Buddhism in particular, we found that, at its foundation, we clearly have both the ideal of the bodhisattva, one who tries to committedly realize the salvation of others, and also the high-level philosophies of emptiness and Buddha-nature. However, despite these, or perhaps *because* of these ideals and philosophies, the principles of ethics end up getting muddled, if not lost sight of altogether.

These foundational concepts show us the gaps in the domain of *ningen*. Not all of our problems can be covered by ethics. Thus there is a demand to take a leap from ethics to the trans-ethical. However, we should not ignore the problems of ethics either. Here, I would like to touch upon a form of Buddhism that actively commits to engaging socio-ethical problems.

Primarily in Southeast Asia, we see a movement wherein people actively speak and do social practice in response to social problems from a Buddhist standpoint. Not only are people in Europe and America beginning to pay attention to this phenomenon and conduct research on it, but Buddhists and Buddhist scholars in the west are beginning to take part in this movement as well. This movement is called "Engaged Buddhism." Unfortunately, it has not been sufficiently introduced to Japan and is not well-known here. It is so poorly understood that the standard Japanese translation for "Engaged Buddhism" has yet to be decided. Recently, a young researcher named Ranjana Mukhopadhyaya published a book entitled *Socially Engaged Buddhism in Japan*.[20] Here, she used the translation *Shakai sanka Bukkyō* (lit. society + join + Buddhism),[21] and I think that is a good translation.

This phrase was originally coined by Thích Nhất Hạnh from Vietnam. Nhất Hạnh is a monk who led the anti-war movement against the Vietnam war. Part of his group was Thích Quảng Đức (known for setting himself on fire in protest).

The most canonical, well-known work about Buddhism is a word edited by Christopher S. Queen and Sallie B. King, *Engaged Buddhism: Buddhist Liberation Movements in Asia*, which takes up the new Buddhist movement of Ambedkar in India, A. T. Ariyaratne in Sri Lanka, the monk Buddhadasa Bhikkhu in Thailand, Sulak Sivaraksa, also in Thailand, Dalai Lama's activities in Tibet, and Thích Nhất Hạnh in Vietnam.[22]

In this book, Daniel A. Metraux takes up Soka Gakkai as an example of Engaged Buddhism in Japan. For certain, in Japan, it was mostly the new religions, or relatively new religious groups, that actively developed social movements. The movements of the original Buddhist groups are considerably delayed. In Mukhopadhyaya's book that I just mentioned, she also mostly discusses the new religious groups like Risshō Kōsei-kai.

Furthermore, in modern China, Taixu and his disciple Yinshun advocated "Humanistic Buddhism" (C. *renjian fojiao*). "Humanistic" refers to secular society, and is thus similar to the word "*ningen*" as I use it in this book. Therefore, "Humanistic Buddhism" is a form of Buddhism that emphasizes social praxis, rather than being cloistered

---

20. Ranjana Mukhopadhyaya, 『日本の社会参加仏教』 [Socially engaged Buddhism in Japan] (Tokyo: Tōshindō, 2005).

21. 社会参加仏教.

22. Christopher S. Queen and Sallie B. King, eds., *Engaged Buddhism: Buddhist Liberation Movements in Asia* (Albany, NY: SUNY Press, 1996).

in temples. The influence of this movement spread across the mainland and to Taiwan. In the mainland, it actively cooperated with the establishment of socialism, and in Taiwan, it gave rise to the Fo Guang Shan and Tzu Chi religious groups. In comparison to these, we would have to say that Japan's large scale Buddhist social activities fall far short.

THE SOCIAL PRAXIS OF BUDDHISTS IN JAPAN

Ama Toshimaro's *Buddhism that Creates Society*[23] offers another translation for Engaged Buddhism in his title, and puts "Engaged Buddhism" (Romanized in Japanese) as his subtitle. This book introduced this largely unknown movement to Japan, and took up Kiyozawa Manshi, Takagi Kenmyō, and their True Pure Land school's movements in the Meiji period as examples of Japanese Engaged Buddhism.

Takagi can certainly be recognized as having the germ of socially engaged Buddhism, and I want to give this further consideration later on. However, while Kiyozawa did participate actively in movements within the sect—the sect reform movement and sect educational reform—and had a religious commune with his disciples called the Kōkōdō (literally "Wide, Expansive Cave"), I think these are properly included in the domain of religion that transcends secular ethics. I believe he established a sense of spiritual freedom unconstrained by statist morals.

Of course, even in Japan, there are a good number of Buddhists who actively tackled social issues: Sakaino Kōyō's Association of New Buddhists, Itō Shōshin's Selfless Love Movement, Nishida Tenkō's One Torch Park, Seno'o Girō's Youth Movement for Revitalizing Buddhism, and, in the postwar, people like Fujii Nittatsu's peace movement, etc. The awareness of social issues and practical social move-

---

23. Ama Toshimaro 阿満利麿『社会を作る仏教』[Buddhism that creates society] (Kyoto: Jinbunshoin, 2003).

ments did develop, and by no means was this direction lacking. Even today, Buddhists are active in the Vihāra movement (Buddhist hospice) and environmental protection movements, and are also carrying out collaborative projects with people outside Japan. However, despite that, the general impression one gets is *not* one of vibrant activity in the field of social ethics. Why is this so?

There are several possible reasons for this. First, one thing we need to consider is that because the aspect of funeral Buddhism is so entrenched in society, other social activities tend to be overshadowed. "Funeral Buddhism" (*sōshiki Bukkyō*) is usually spoken of with a negative nuance. However, while a complacent acceptance of funeral Buddhism is out of the question, I think that it would be problematic if we looked at in a purely negative way. Rather, we should seek the original source of the Japanese way of socially engaged Buddhism that is rooted in this region and its funeral Buddhism.

I will be taking up the issues of funeral Buddhism in the next chapter, so let me move on to another reason here. That second reason is that, in modernity, many of the Buddhist movements were nipped in the bud by statism and emperor-centrism, or else the former were absorbed within the latter, thus losing all criticality. The after effects of this carried over into the post-war period, preventing these Buddhist movements from ever getting back on their feet. We see the severity of circumstances here. This problem has long been an undercurrent in Japan, but save for formalistic criticisms, it has not been dealt with sufficiently.

For instance, in the prewar period, one of the most active leaders of social movements—arguably a prototype for Engaged Buddhism—was Tanaka Chigaku and his National Pillar Association. With works like "A Theory of Buddhist Husband and Wife" and "A Theory of Buddhist Monks [Eating] Meat and Marrying," Chigaku was originally a proponent of laicism and the theory of monks marrying. At the end of the Meiji period, he actively preached the theory of the *kokutai* (national entity/polity), and with emperor-centrism and Nichirenism as his two pillars, he promoted militant proselytization. However, because of this, he became taboo in the post-war period, and until very recently, nobody dared to do serious research on him.

Furthermore, aiming to establish a national system of ordination, he worked out a clear theory of the unity of religion and politics, which was a direct challenge to modern theories of the division of church and state. This way of thinking was inherited in the post-war period by Soka Gakkai and became quite a force. But despite that, nobody really took it up academically. Such "dangerous philosophies" were seen as taboo, and people tended to respond to these malodorous matters by covering them up.

THE GRASSROOTS WORK OF TAKAGI KENMYŌ

On the other hand, another factor is that people have tended to avoid proper reconsideration of the Buddhist priests who were implicated in the High Treason Incident in the late Meiji period. The incident occurred in 1910, when certain figures were accused of (supposedly) plotting the assassination of the emperor. Kōtoku Shūsui and other anarchists and socialists were rounded up, and in the next year, Kōtoku and 23 others were sentenced to die. Twelve of them were actually executed, and 12 others had their sentences commuted to life imprisonment. Among those who were executed was the Sōtō Zen priest, Uchiyama Gudō. The True Pure Land priest, (Ōtani sect) Takagi Kenmyō, and the Rinzai Zen priest, (Myōshin-ji sect) Mineo Setsudō, were among those imprisoned for life.

Promptly after receiving the court's decision, these men were all defrocked and expelled by their respective sects. In times like those where such matters were not clarified to the general public, perhaps such expulsions could not have been helped. Nevertheless, it does betray how self-protecting sects were—rushing to put out warnings in each temple not to repeat such scandals, putting inquiries to the Imperial Household Agency, issuing apologies, and so on. In the post-war period, even while these men were cleared from these false charges, the sects put off reinstating them, and their sanctions were not cleared until the 1990s.

Takagi Kenmyō, who was taken up in Ama Toshimaro's book, was active mainly in the Shingū area of Wakayama Prefecture, where he was the priest at a temple called Seisen-ji (Temple of the Pure Spring). Takagi was active in the *buraku* liberation movement and in the protests against licensed prostitution. During the Russo-Japanese war, he took an anti-war stance, and criticized the jingoism that was widespread in the Buddhist world. From his philosophy, he joined the group of socialist Ōishi Seinosuke in Shingū and began his contact with Kōtoku Shūsui and his group.

Takagi's philosophy is clearly written in a short tract called "I'm Socialist." There he writes, "I think that socialism is closely related to religion, rather than politics." It is clear that his standpoint is purely religious. Without relying on preexisting theories, he constructed his philosophy of praxis on the basis of his own faith. From there, Takagi preached the equality of *Namu Amida Butsu* (the chant of pledging one's reliance on Amitābha), and emphasized that Sukhā-vatī, Amitābha's paradise, is an ideal world that realizes socialism, and that one cannot extract a support for war from anywhere in the faith in Amitābha. From the vantage point of the present, this may seem like a decent philosophy with nothing strange about it. But what is frightening is how quickly it was stamped out and for how long it was forgotten.

What is worth noting with Takagi is that he lived in the thick of it as the chief priest of a temple and practiced in the *genba*—the place where the action is—to the very end. Even his engagement with the problem of *buraku* discrimination was because many of his parishio-ners in Seisen-ji were *buraku* people, and it was thus a problem born from actual everyday life. It was not a vain philosophy of borrowed ideas, but rather, he tried to take a stance from his own faith and thor-oughgoing grassroots praxis. There is much we can learn from him today. It is important to think of global, large-scale problems. But I think it is more important to have a philosophy that is not divorced from where one lives—a philosophy with both feet on the ground.

9

What's Wrong with Funeral Buddhism?

Today, the most common relationship most average Japanese have with Buddhist temples is usually something related to funerals and memorial services. Temples do not have much of a relationship with everyday life otherwise. This form of Buddhism is called "funeral Buddhism," a phrase often said with a sneer.

Funeral Buddhism generally has a bad reputation. One has to pay a posthumous Buddhist name fee and give "alms" (more like a sizable donation), just to have someone chant a few sutras. Things would be much clearer if temples clearly spelled out the costs and gave receipts, but rather, while claiming that "Whatever the believer deigns to give will do," one gets a sour face and a sarcastic "this one is lacking in faith," if one makes the mistake of giving too little. No matter where one goes, one can overhear the same badmouthing of temples—that they are pompous, put on airs, give a terrible impression, etc. What on earth happened to the "profound" Buddhist philosophy since India?

I do not have any ties to temples or anything of the sort, but because I am a Buddhist specialist by profession, I often meet with people from temples, whether I like it or not. In the course of these interactions, I have found that being a temple priest is quite a challenging job, and I cannot simply badmouth them anymore. In a large religious organization, their specific rules and customs are quite complex, and there are things that would make no sense to those in the corporate world. But on the other hand, since they have to deal with parishioners as well, I hear that the very attempt to abide by one's conscience can be a cause for much distress. There is a reason why temple children do not want to take over the temple. I myself would never dream of working at a temple. Had I been born to a family that runs a temple, I probably would have run away.

Today, if one goes to countries like China, one finds that temples deal with such diverse enterprises as to merit being called "businesses." Particularly in Taiwan, temple activities are vibrant and large scale. The activities of Taiwanese Buddhist groups are, from Japanese eyes, similar to new religious movements. Through the charisma of their leaders, the circle of the activities of the faithful who gather around the leader gradually expands.

In contrast, Japanese Buddhism is characterized by small temples that are the size of a family, located in a city or a village, which carry out their activities rooted in a particular place. Thus, the chief priest of a temple is a businessman of sorts, who is tied to a particular region. On that point, it is no different from other professions. Rather, that way of being is so ordinary that it is hard for a Japanese person to imagine any other form for it. However, despite this ordinariness, this form is quite peculiar to Japan and cannot be found in Buddhism elsewhere.

I see this peculiar form of Buddhism in Japan as having two factors: First, it is a form of Buddhism that takes funeral Buddhism as its core and thus centers on the social function of funerals and memorial services for the dead. Second, in this Buddhism, priests get married and thus the temple can be passed on by blood relations.

THE POTENTIAL OF FUNERAL BUDDHISM

Let us start by considering the first factor. The involvement of Buddhists in memorial services for the dead can be seen ever since the early stages of the transmission of Buddhism, and can be seen in the Buddhism of other countries leading up to its arrival in Japan. But unique to Japan is the phenomenon wherein this function of Buddhism became the main function. This traces all the way back to the Edo period (1603–1868). Even in the Muromachi period (1333–1573), there were many sermons on funerals and memorial services included in the records of Zen priests, and the gradual turn to funeral Buddhism is well-known. However, it was in the Edo period that the temple registry system came about.

The temple registry system was originally for residents to prove that they were not Christians, during the time of the ban against Christianity. They created sect registries, which also served the function of a census. In this way, the temple registry system used temples as an administrative organ extending up to the furthest reaches of the Edo shogunate. While temples carried out this function efficiently, this function became the foundation for the very existence of these temples. Amidst this, temples became connected not merely with the living but with the maintenance of cemeteries, the death register—the census for the dead—thus carrying out its role vis-à-vis the dead. Then, the activities of temples became more and more dependent on "funeral Buddhism," which is centered on funerals and memorial services for the deceased.

Given that the temple registry system was enforced by the policies of the Edo shogunate, it seemed like the activities of temples would be liberated and the system dismantled with the collapse of the shogunate. But that was not to be the case. The temple registry system remained, even in the Meiji period and beyond, and the funeral Buddhism centered on memorial services lived on. Therefore, one cannot make the excuse that funeral Buddhism, founded on the temple registry system, was caused entirely by political enforcement in the Edo period. Rather, this form lives on due to the fit between the needs of temples and parishioners.

Some Shintoists realized that so long as funeral rites and ceremonies were entrusted to Buddhists, the power of Buddhism would endure. So they tried to kick-start a "Shinto funeral movement," and tried to spread Shinto-style funeral services and memorial services. But this was only picked up by a small segment of society, and most people remained unmoved by this. This shows us how entrenched funeral Buddhism is in Japan.

Of course, just because things are as above does not mean that the form of funeral Buddhism as it has continued up to the present can merely continue, as it is, into the future. Funeral Buddhism, since the parishioner system, has closely depended on the *ie* (house) system and thus retained its power. However, with the normative power of the house system quickly dwindling with the growth of individual consciousness, the survival of the parishioner system itself has become questionable. Funerals and graves are no longer a must; individuals are now free to choose various forms for these things. For sure, this will impact the shape of Buddhism considerably.

Some would argue that funeral Buddhism is therefore wrong and that only by getting rid of it can we recover authentic Buddhism. Despite the premises being true, that conclusion seems off the mark, does it not? With the progress of Buddhist studies, people came to know the original scriptures of Indian Buddhism. With that, Japanese people tended to criticize Japanese Buddhism, particularly funeral Buddhism, from the standpoint of this "original Buddhism." Many argued that Japanese Buddhism is a mere "expedient means" (*hōben*) and not the real Buddhism. However, while this view that negates funeral Buddhism may seem valid at first glance (or perhaps this is just the self-effacing of Japanese Buddhists), it is a bit too simplistic. It disposes of Japanese Buddhism without sufficiently considering the particular form which Japanese Buddhists have built up over the ages.

Of course, I am not saying that funeral Buddhism is fine the way it is. We Japanese need to expand the possibilities for forms of Buddhism beyond this funeral-centered one. But what meaning is there behind the long historical endurance and social fixity of funeral Buddhism? Without giving that due thought, it is not quite right to make light of it and just ditch it. Relating to the dead opens the door to a new world that transcends the superficial ethics of the living. I shall be developing this line of thought throughout this book.

How the permission of meat-eating and marriage secularized monks

The second characteristic of Japanese Buddhism is that priests can get married and have families. Because of this, temples are often passed on to children as one would private property.

This form was authorized at the start of the Meiji period, after funeral Buddhism began. By official government decree, priests were permitted to eat meat and marry starting 1871. Until that point, it was only priests of the True Pure Land school who, following the footsteps of their founder Shinran, were permitted to marry. All the other sects had to obey the precepts and sexual relations with women were forbidden. But this was in principle, as they say in Japanese, *tatemae*. In actuality, many were married or at the least having relations with women. As such, the official permit for marriage in 1871 was received in the Buddhist world without much fuss. But the actual institutional permission of marriage had an extremely large significance for the social position of Buddhism.

What sort of significance? Because priests were permitted to eat meat and marry, legally, they became absolutely no different from the average citizen. Certainly, it was common for monks, even in the Edo period, to live quite secular lives. However, they existed outside the four classes (samurai, farmers, artisans, and merchants), and matters concerning monks and temples were the jurisdiction of the Jishabugyō (shogunate arm for temple and shrine affairs). So theirs was an existence quite different from the average layperson. However, with the permission for marriage, the special characteristics of monks ceased to be a legal concern, and their profession was treated the same as other professions.

Speaking of 1871, the religious policies of the government were placed under the charge of the Ministry of Religious Education, and the previous Department of Divinities and Ministry of Divinities were changed and given educational duties. It was a time when new state policies concerning religion were being adopted, and Buddhism got caught up in this as well. The policy on meat-eating and marriage of monks was born as Buddhism tried to come to grips with state policies in this period of change. No longer were monks there to save people while standing outside the secular world. Rather, they were tasked with serving the state, as one part of society bearing the duty of the state's educational policies. In 1868, Fukuda Gyōkai and others advocated the revival of the precepts, and there were movements that sought to strictly maintain the precepts and thus revitalize Buddhism. But despite these, with the permission of meat-eating and marriage, such movements were totally abandoned.

The religious policies of the Ministry of Religious Education eventually triggered a backlash from the True Pure Land school (because of ill-faring attempts to involve Buddhism in state policy via the establishment of integrated religious training centers) resulting in the failure of the policies. But the policy on meat-eating and marriage of monks was never to be reversed. From a legal standpoint, monks had become completely secularized. And Japanese Buddhism was to develop an unprecedented unique form—what could be called "secular Buddhism." One can also say that this was a shift away from Catholicism, which forbids the marriage of priests, toward a protestant form of religion, wherein pastors are allowed to marry.

There was no way for this *not* to influence the ethics of Buddhists. The fundamental role of "otherworldly" Buddhist priests, wherein they adhered to the precepts, and standing in a sacred world transcending the profane, extended salvation to the laity, could no longer hold. Rather, they lived their lives in the same secular level as "householders," troubled by the same concerns as the laity, taking pleasure from the same joys as the laity, and forced to think about Buddhism from within society itself. It is because of this same background that a good deal of modern Buddhist thought was carried out by laypersons, who in turn influenced the world of priests.

However, despite all this, there are problems in Buddhism that cannot be completely embedded within the secular. People turn to religion in order seek something that cannot be resolved merely by the secular. But what might that be? It is in the space beyond the ethics of the secular world where the real problems begin.

Part Two

From *Ningen* to the Other

10

Ningen as the Foundation of Ethics

Up to this point, we have considered how the problems of ethics can be addressed from within the framework of Buddhism. Ethics was definitely possible in early Buddhism, and there is legitimacy in contemporary forms like Engaged Buddhism as well. However, in the core principles of Mahāyāna Buddhism, there are elements that muddle ethics itself, and there are problems suggested that cannot be solved by ethics—trans-ethical problems. When we drift beyond the orbit of ethics, there we encounter the other. The question of how to come to terms with the other is one of the greatest problems of the trans-ethical. Given this, from this point on I will still be keeping the Buddhist tradition in mind, but I will not let myself get caught up in it. Rather, from a more general standpoint, I wish to think about ethics and its limits, and how the trans-ethical, which transgresses the bounds of the ethical, might come about.

For instance, let us consider the general rule, "Thou shalt not kill." I cannot say with certainty that this applies universally, but at any rate, this rule is quite widely accepted, and it is one of the fundamental laws of ethics. What I wish to pose here is, from what sort of a basis is this being asserted? This most famously appeared in Moses' Ten Commandments, but there, it is given by God, making our consent and refusal quite irrelevant. Although I hear that in Old Testament studies, one cannot just simply declare that its normativity is based on its having been given by God. I will leave that discussion for elsewhere.

The same rule comes up as the first of the five precepts of Buddhism. In its original conception in India, people were restricted from killing not only people but animals as well. According to the theory of *saṃsāra*, humans can be born as animals (in a future life), so there was a sense of equality between human beings and other animals. From the period of early Buddhism, there was a practice called *vārṣika*, wherein monks spent the rainy season in only one place, meditating. They did this not because it was hard to move around when the weather was bad but because the possibility of accidentally trampling to death the larvae born in water puddles was high. Taken to an extreme, one could say that the act of breathing itself takes in microbes (and kills some of them), and is thus wrong. This would result in a rigid doctrine like Jainism, where starving to death is taken to be ideal.

At any rate, why do we have to abide by the precept of not killing? Circumstances are different for laity and for monks. In the case of monks, adherence to the precepts is the first step on the path of spiritual practice, as is said in the three learnings (or the three parts of the noble eightfold path, moral conduct or *śīla*, meditation or *samādhi*, and wisdom or *prajñā*).

For laypersons, good conduct in abiding by the precepts is for the sake of improving one's chances to be reborn in heaven or to receive other positive karmic fruits. As the saying goes: Good cause, pleasurable effect; bad cause, painful effect.[1] If one does good things, one will have happiness, but if one does evil deeds, it will bring misfortune. The principle of karmic retribution can be seen in all parts of the world, but if we think of it in terms of this life alone, such a principle cannot be consistently upheld. Just as there are people who do good things but live miserable lives, there are those who do terrible things but manage to live quite happy lives until the end. In order to solve this problem, we have to consider future lives. As such, the principle of *saṃsāra* is rational to the extreme. The Christian idea of the final judgment day is another solution, but it only occurs once, unlike transmigration.

---

1. 善因楽果; 悪因苦果.

There are other theories, outside of the above mentioned, that ground ethics and morality. We can divide them in two: First are the karmic explanations that have to do with seeking a positive consequence, and second are those that, regardless of consequence, assert the imperative of people doing good. Fundamentally, one goes by either of these.

The latter does not seek compensation, but rather argues that humans have a will to goodness, which is a sentiment that inevitably arises from within. The Christian love for humankind is an example of this. Kant's argument for a priori moral law is another. In China, the theory of fundamental goodness of human nature in the *Mencius* is the classic case, and came to clash with the theory of fundamental evil in *Xunzi*, which argued for the need for heteronomous regulation. The former way of thinking (mentioned in the previous paragraph) that tries to guide people through incentives, and the notion of karmic retribution is a type of this. If we think of this on the level of this life, then it becomes what we call "utilitarianism." Here, the notion of one becoming happy because one does good is diverted, and, rather than being thought of from the level of individuals alone, it turns toward the pursuit of the interests of the social collective. This is the principle of "the greatest happiness of the greatest number."

Watsuji's "ethics as the study of *ningen*"

Let me put aside the criticism of these moral theories in order to consider something that comes from a completely different dimension, a most interesting theory put forth by the Japanese ethicist Watsuji Tetsurō (1889–1960).

Basically, western moral philosophies grasp individuals as standing alone, and see society as the result of putting together these scattered autonomous individuals. Even if they abide by the principle of the greatest happiness of the greatest number, if individuals merely pursue their own interests, they would end up at each other's throats.

This necessitates regulation, thus showing that this principle still takes individuals as its base.

In contrast to that approach, Watsuji emphasizes how every human being is, from the beginning, thrown into society. To begin with, the word *ningen* (human) is written with the characters for "between persons."[2] In other words, a human is, from the very start, born "between persons," and the notion of an isolated (or self-standing) human being is no more than a fiction. *Ningen* is an existence that is "between persons" (or "inter-personal"),[3] a relational existence where people bear some sort of mutual connection with each other.

Originally, the word *renjian* in Chinese meant the world, the realm where people dwell. It did not have the meaning of "an individual human being" like it does in Japanese. Watsuji cleverly picked up on the duality of the word *ningen / renjian*, and named his own ethical theory as "Ethics as the Study of *Ningen*." And from this theory, he tackled the different forms of "the betweenness of persons," from the small-scale (families) to the large (states). In other words, ethics is not something that "ought to be," on the basis of some special principle. Rather, ethics is the pattern of action that *ningen*, as an existence "between persons," naturally abides by. Ethics consists of the rules that make "the betweenness of persons" possible.

Such a view that emphasizes the collective can also be found in the Japanese folklore studies that began with Yanagita Kunio. Japanese folklore studies idealizes agricultural villages and studies the customs and habits found therein. It is dangerous to immediately call these approaches "typically Japanese," but arguably, both Watsuji and

2. 人の間.

3. [*Hito no aida* is a key term in this book. As a modifier (人の間的), it can be rendered as "inter-personal" (with the dash to differentiate it from its ordinary usage as in *taijin* 対人) or as "between persons." As a noun, it refers to the space between that connects people, and is usually rendered as the "betweenness of persons." Thus being "between" and being "beyond / trans" are placed in tension with each other, resulting in the contrasting pair of "inter-personal ethics" and "trans-ethics."]

Yanagita analyzed the human way of existence based on the model of Japanese agricultural society. In prewar Japan, even the state was often considered an extension of the family or the town community.

The communities of old do not necessarily remain today. Because of this, there is no guarantee of the applicability of Watsuji's system. However, I think we can still consider as applicable the core idea that *ningen* is an existence "between persons." From the birth of an infant, it matures within its relationship with its parents and within society (which includes even those outside the parent-child relation). It does not just grow up all by itself. And therein, we can be sure that there will be rules to make the "betweenness of persons" possible. The maturation of a child is not merely the enlargement of the body, but is in mastering these rules. The good part of this way of thinking is that it becomes possible to think about ethics while omitting the transcendent that goes beyond the betweenness of persons (like gods or transmigration). Ethics in the domain of *ningen*, which I have mentioned often in this book, is of this sort.

Ethics as the rules "between persons"

The inter-personal has many possible forms. Even within filial relations alone, we have parental, spousal, in-law relations, and so on. We also have friends, teachers and students. In corporate life, we have subordinates and superiors, colleagues, and clients. This "betweenness of persons" is also present between anonymous people jostling against each other in a rush-hour train. Beyond direct contact, with political and economic activities, one might even say that some sort of relationship is formed amongst all the people on the planet. Depending on each inter-personal relationship, the rules differ, and these entangle with each other in a rather complex way.

By making these rules explicit, we have laws. Furthermore, we have complex, institutionalized relationships like the systems of politics and economics. On the other hand, at the furthermost margins of the domain of rules, we have things like customs, which somehow make sense to those within the group (albeit in an unarticulated way). There are also minute rules restricted to a particular parent and child or pair of lovers. There are both rules that must be obeyed without exception, and lighter rules that do not need to be strictly adhered to. For instance, if there is a rule that lovers kiss each other goodbye, in a case that this *does not* happen, then perhaps things are not quite normal between the two.

Of course, it is a bit forced if we swap the word ethics for rules. Typical examples of rules are the regulations of a sport. But for example, when we say that one ought to follow the rules in baseball, it is completely different from saying that the team must do its best to win *with a sense of responsibility*. So for instance, if one misses one's chance with an easy ball and strikes out, rule-wise there is no issue. But ethically (and this may be said without overstatement), one will probably take flak for not trying hard enough. However, if we think of rules in a broader sense, we can also say that doing one's best for one's team to win is one of the rules that makes baseball work. If one deliberately commits an error in order to cause one's team to lose, the game itself becomes impossible, and one probably could not even consider that person as a member of the team.

We can think of "thou shalt not kill" as one of these inter-personal rules. As such, it is only when this rule is "in circulation" that it holds—it is not a universal principle that is justified everywhere. For example, this rule does not hold in a battlefield. This rule stands in peaceful civil society, on the condition that one's life is not in danger. In a gun-toting society like the United States of America, citizens have guns in order to defend themselves. If their lives are in danger, they will be allowed to fire on others, and that is seen as a quite natural thing. As such, there is no universal ethics. All ethics come to be in response to circumstances. It is unthinkable to have a person living alone, isolated from circumstance.

Against this, perhaps there are those who would argue that right is right, regardless of all circumstances. But actually, in the world today, we have the tragedy occurring everywhere, wherein both sides assert that they are right and fight against each other. However, who can decide which side is truly right? Perhaps at the end of the day, that is no more than a belief, with no objective foundation whatsoever. An ethics that ignores circumstances is bound to fail.

11

Deviating from *Ningen*

As inter-personal, the being of human beings takes the form of mutual *relations*. Furthermore, it is rules that constitute *ningen* as relations. The biological parent-child relationship does not make up the parent-child relationship (as *ningen*) on its own. Although the biological part of the parent-child relationship endures despite a parent abandoning his / her child, the parent-child relationship as a *ningen* relationship ceases to exist. Child-rearing is a rule of *ningen* that governs a parent vis-à-vis a child (at least in most societies).

These relatively clear relationships are not the only ones which have rules—we have them too even between strangers walking past each other. There are circumstances wherein you can greet complete strangers, "*konnichiwa*." But in a big metropolis, if you greet someone like that, he or she would probably be quite unnerved.

When we think of ethics as inter-personal rules, one characteristic of it is that rules can be explained linguistically. Of course, not all rules are actually linguistically articulated, and a good number of them are only tacitly understood. However, even so, there must be a way to articulate these into verbal stipulations. Otherwise, it would be impossible to judge which acts abide by the rules and which deviate from them. "If you tell me, I will understand," is a core principle of rule-bound society.

Although rules may not be directly expressed in language, for instance in the case of a farewell kiss between lovers, it is understood as expressing the health of their relationship and as a sign meaning, "I'll see you again." Even a trifling matter such as whether or not one greets a stranger "*konnichiwa*" can express friendliness or hostility. In this way, one can see that the society we live in is linguistically articulated and made meaningful. The process of a child coming to remember rules is the same as the process of a child coming to remember words.

In this way, we live in a linguistically articulated world, and people and things come to bear meanings. For example, let us consider the case of a businessman. When he goes into a company, he is given a clear position of being Mr. X from Sales, Section Manager Y's subordinate, etc. The rules for how he should act are defined as well. When he comes home, he is his wife's husband, and his children's parent. Just because he has gone home does not mean he can just relax.

THE INTER-PERSONAL RULES ARE SUBJECT TO CHANGE

In this way, the domain of *ningen* is like a mesh. In it, we are mutually determined by "relations," and there are given rules as to how we should act. However, despite that, the domain of *ningen* does have exceptions. Certainly, Japan spent a long time as an agricultural society with relatively high social stability and little change. A village had, to a certain extent, a closed structure. In such a society, as mutual relations were difficult to change, rules were relatively clearly fixed.

However, the idea of a closed society transcending time is completely abstract and is not possible in reality. In contrast to the fixed village, the city has, from a relatively early period, been a fluid space. In such a place, the notion of "relations" that held currency in villages no longer holds true. The Edo period tried to reduce social change by limiting the mobility of the populace, but the monetary economy quickly developed and preexisting relations started to crumble. Amidst the economic power relations of the survival of the fittest, the rules of relations began to change. However, as society changed, new rules were created. Rules are not unchanging, but rather, they transform from era to era.

Although in the blistering pace of social change in the past few years, not unexpectedly, it is the rules that have had difficulty catching up. From scientific issues like great global-scale environmental catastrophes and the engineering of life itself, to the more intimate level of the household, it no longer makes sense what sort of rules hold sway. What sort of "relations" can hold true in the "betweenness of persons?" It has gotten quite vague. Moreover, along with the globalization of society, we have groups with different value systems crashing headlong into each other. Society is also complexifying, and there are many cases wherein each person needs to take on several differing senses of values in a layered fashion. Given this, we have arrived at a situation for which *ningen*, as the notion of the inter-personal within a relatively simple social model, can no longer account for.

In the first place, the "betweenness of persons" can arise only when people mutually recognize relations and rules. Taking it from the baseball rules I previously mentioned, a game cannot take place unless everyone recognizes that three strikes are an out. If one plays overseriously and refuses to leave the mound until one has made a successful hit, the game will not move. People like that get kicked out of the game.

If it were just a game, then even if it did not proceed well, or even if one got ejected from the game, then so what. But things are quite serious when we are talking about the problems of society. For example, there can be people who refuse to acknowledge even the rule "thou shalt not kill," which holds currency in most civil societies, or do not care if they are punished for violating it. If there are people like that, the rules do not hold them down. What do terrorists care about rules? If a global superpower insists on being belligerent, how can we stop them? Thinking of it like this, we can see how "the betweenness of persons" is quite at risk.

However, despite that, if we critically examine this issue from another angle, destroying the "betweenness of persons" itself is no simple task. If a minority raises opposition against the rule "thou shalt not kill," and breaks that rule, then unless there is something radical behind such an opposition, the rule stays and its tears are mended. If we mutually define our roles through words, then a new "relationship" is born. After war, after calamity, rather than falling into chaos, people have created new relations and new rules. There, a public space is inaugurated, and argumentation and coordination are made possible.

What cannot be said

Every nook and cranny of our world is given meaning and order by language. I think that is a splendid thing. However, there is a bit of an annoyance here. Let us take the example of me, alone in a room, completely absorbed in thinking. Even in this case, so long as I am using words, my speculations are open to a public space. Although I may secretly keep a journal entirely for myself alone, these words are the words of the "betweenness of persons." If so, is there such a thing as genuine solitariness? Words penetrate deep, deep into us.

But despite this, is there not something that escapes this publicization? Something mine alone, an experience I cannot share with others—that would be, ultimately, something that cannot be turned into words, something that cannot be expressed. Is there really such a thing? It is said, for example, that the extreme experience of enlightenment is ineffable. Is that really so?

Although this may be a bit abrupt, allow me to introduce here an episode that transpires in the *Mencius*. In the kingdom of Qi, there was a king called Xuan. One day, the king saw people pulling an ox. When he asked his retainers where they were bringing it, they explained that they were bringing it in order to sacrifice it at a festival. Looking at the cowering beast, the king took pity and ordered them to spare it. But it would not do to cancel the festival either. It was decided that instead of the ox, they would use a sheep. However, a rumor began to circulate amongst the people that the reason why a small sheep was used instead of an ox was that the king was being stingy.

Against this, Mencius says:

> This itself is a precious act of *rén* (humanity, authoritative conduct).
> While he had seen the ox, he had not seen the sheep. Though it be a bird
> or a beast, seeing it as living, one cannot bear to see it slain. Hearing it
> cry out [piteously, as it is slain], one cannot have the appetite to eat its
> flesh. Thus is human feeling. Therefore, the *junzi* (superior or wise per-
> son) does not place his living room near the kitchen.[4]

Mencius says it is the feeling of being unable to bear to watch a
living being be slain that is the beginning of morality. That is probably
true, but is it not a bit hypocritical? Saying that one cannot bear to kill
the ox one has seen, but that it is fine to kill the sheep one has not—
that would be quite selfish. Because of this, I thought that *Mencius* was
the embodiment of feudal morality, and I could not bring myself to
like it at all.

THE DOMAIN INEXPRESSIBLE BY PUBLIC SPEECH

However, when I read the French philosopher François
Jullien, who takes up the same story in *Fonder la morale: Dialogue de
Mencius avec un philosophe des Lumieres* (1995), it struck me that per-
haps a serious problem lies concealed here. Jullien writes:

> The king saw with his own eyes that one fearful beast. Because that
> surprise appeared before him unexpectedly, he had no time to prepare
> himself. However, another animal's life was for him no more than an
> idea.... Because it was the ox that he had seen, the king was moved, and
> his internal logic was instantly shaken.[5]

4. 「梁惠王上」[King Liang of Hui, I] 『孟子』[Mencius], trans. by Kobayashi Katsundo
小林勝人 (Tokyo: Iwanami Bunko, 1968), sec. 7. See James Legge and Arthur Waley, *The
Works of Mencius* (Hong Kong: Hong Kong University Press, 1960).

5. François Jullien, trans. by Nakajima Takahiro 中島隆博 and Shino Yoshinobu 志野
好伸『道徳を基礎づける：孟子vsカント、ルソー、ニーチェ』[Founding morality: Mencius
vs. Kant, Rousseau, Nietzsche] (Tokyo: Kōdansha Gendai Shinsho, 2002), 21–22. See
François Jullien, *Dialogue sur la morale* (Paris: Le Livre de Poche, 1998).

In our everyday lives, there often things that we would have been better off not seeing. This is not a problem so long as it is only to an extent that allows for a quick recovery of the everyday. So long as that is the case, we return to the order of the "betweenness of persons" without issue. However, if the shock is too great, things cannot be put back together through public words. Auschwitz, Hiroshima, the great Hanshin earthquake (1995), 9/11—to see this is one's tragedy. In moments like these, it is as if one can no longer speak with innocence; and the unspeakable precipitates as trauma.

It does not have to be a big, world-historical event. There are things which strike me, and me alone, deeply, leaving scars, like the pain, suffering, and sorrow we experience in our everyday lives. There is no way to explain these things away. With these, no amount of sympathy or consolation have any power.

There are things that cannot be said. If so, we cannot remain within the level of relational *ningen*, on the level of public speech. What do we see when we go beyond the domain of *ningen*? It is as if ethics can no longer hold sway. Here, we are compelled to grapple with the problems of "religion," as the trans-ethical that is irreducible to ethics.

12

The Discovery of the Other and Religion

If all problems could be resolved within the domain of *ningen*, there would be no issue. However, whether we like it or not, we cannot help but come into relation with matters that spill beyond the domain of *ningen*, issues we cannot find rational explanations for. This occurs even in the midst of the banalities of everyday life. It is here where the sphere of religion begins.

At this point, let us briefly review the notion of ethics one more time. Ethics holds sway in the domain of *ningen* which is inter-personal. People do not exist isolated, nor do we begin with disconnected individuals gathered in a completely chaotic state, and then from there come up with a social contract. People are, from their birth, in the "betweenness of persons," and they are raised and educated in order to be able to live in this betweenness. Ethics is made up of the rules that allow this betweenness of persons to stand. These inter-personal rules are expressed in a shared language by members.

In a society that is closed and stable to a certain degree, inter-personal rules operate smoothly. However, if society undergoes a great change, or if it begins relating with another society with different rules, then the rules become rather unclear. In such a situation, rules with a higher commonality become necessary. In this way, a universal public space is formed as an ideal. The various sciences, politics, laws, economics, etc., which all use language, are made possible in such a public space.

However, not all problems can be solved within this "betweenness of persons," within this shared space expressed by language and regulated by rules. There are problems that cannot be fully contained therein, that deviate from betweenness. To begin with, these rules themselves are not really as solid as they seem.

HOW CAN ETHICS DEAL WITH THE INCOMPREHENSIBLE OTHER?

This is a bit of an extreme case, but the philosopher Saul Aaron Kripke thought up a strange mathematical operation called "quus." He defines it as follows:

x quus y = x + y, if x, y < 57
= 5 otherwise.
Given that, 13 quus 24 = 37, but 243 quus 389 = 5.[6]

When a grade school teacher teaches addition, what he teaches is "plus," not "quus." However, strictly speaking, when one is counting with small numbers below 57, we cannot tell if students are understanding it as "plus" and not as "quus." When the teacher gives problems whose numbers exceed 57, students might panic and suddenly start throwing out fives. In such a case, one cannot simply just say that the students are wrong. They might have interpreted the teacher's "plus" as "quus," and in that case their answers would be consistent. One cannot rest assured just by knowing we have exceeded 57. It might be when you exceed 100 that you hit "quus." Or maybe 1000.

It might seem like a rather whimsical scenario, but because there is a stage when children cannot comprehend numbers exceeding 10 (the number of their fingers), it is not an entirely meaningless example. To put it conversely, even though the conventions that one knows have been used in society up to this point, perhaps at a certain point, those will turn into "quus" deviations as well. That fear becomes all-perva-

6. See Noya Shigeki 野矢茂樹『心と他者』[Heart-mind and the other] (Tokyo: Keisō Shobō, 1995), 173.

sive. "The possibility that I myself will be branded a *deviant*, by those around me, opens with every step of the application of rules."[7]

Then, if you were the only one going by quus and everyone else was going by the rules of "plus," you would definitely be a deviant. But if there were a group of people all following quus, then perhaps the plus group and the quus group could match each other with some equality. It would be grand if the plus group and the quus group could understand each other's rules. Otherwise, each would assert that their group alone is right, and they would fall into a conflict that would be impossible to resolve. Perhaps a universal public space is nothing more than a dream.

Only when people can be considered as all abiding by the same rules can mutual understanding between people flow unimpeded. However, if there is someone who cannot abide by them, one becomes strongly conscious of heterogeneity. Samukawa Nekomochi writes, "When the story of Tokushima [lit. the island of Toku] reached its climax, there was someone who asked, 'which island are you talking about?'" In life, this happens rather often, and things get real awkward. I myself mess things up a lot, since I do not read situations well.

If it is only to this extent, then we can get by with little harm done. But if someone suddenly jumps up with a knife, well the rules go to hell, so to speak. This is hardly impossible. In 2001, the now indicted Takuma Mamoru barged into Ikeda Elementary School in Osaka and killed eight children. Until the end, he refused to apologize to the bereaved, and, by his own will, received capital punishment. If one regrets his or her sins and apologizes, things are still reducible to within the sphere of rules. Capital punishment can only be punishment because of the understanding that even offenders have this desire not to die. If not even this holds true, execution becomes pointless.

Perhaps this example was too extreme. But be that as it may, the optimistic idea that people can understand things as fellow human

7. Ibid., 175.

beings no longer holds water. When the rules of community are broken, a person then appears as an unintelligible *other*. So long as there is intelligibility—as in cases where someone is a friend, a family member, a teacher, a student—then mutual relations can be clear. Even in the case of strangers riding the same train, the relationship of "stranger" is quite clear. However, when one cannot fit into any of these given relationships, one transforms into the *other*. In such a case, neither the rules of ethics nor law nor politics hold sway. How do we deal with the appearance of the other? Do we have no choice but to exclude the other, to make it as if the other had never existed? However, so long as there is a victim who is slain, a trace that cannot be effaced lingers.

The other, irreducible to rules, unintelligible, is not merely external; it lurks even within oneself. Although one can see the face of another, one cannot see one's own face. Perhaps we understand ourselves least of all. We ourselves cannot tell what sort of actions our inner feelings might trigger.

For example, you love your child. That is fine, but moving on, what if you begin to detest another child who is better off than yours? What if you detest that child's parents, even to the point that you want to kill someone? Amidst these gradually shifting feelings, it is rather difficult to draw the line and judge between which feelings are alright, and which feelings have gone astray.

Or perhaps we could raise a more subtle example. Child abuse does not necessarily occur because the parents do not love the child. Even if one loves one's child, what if one still lashes out at him/her? Is not this very uncontrollable self the greatest of "others?"

Religion is a deviation from the world of *ningen*, but adapts to it

Fundamentally speaking, religion refers to that which relates with those things that deviate from *ningen*; it relates with the *other*. More so, religion itself is a kind of deviation. On that point, reli-

gion is akin to madness, crime, sex, death, passion, and impulse. There
is a reason why religious acts tend to swerve into deviations that are
often rejected by the world of *ningen*. The distinction that Aum Shinrikyō (also known as Aleph) is a false religion, whereas Buddhism is a
true religion, is, after all, no more than the conceit of Buddhists.

In the *Bhagavad Gītā*, India's greatest religious classic, a god took
on a terrible form and swallowed up people. "I am the great time that
will destroy the world. I have begun to act, in order that all worlds
may return to nothingness. Although you may be absent, none of the
soldiers in the opposing army will survive."[8] Gods do not bring happiness alone. Theirs is an existence that inspires awe, bringing death and
destruction as well.

However, let us suppose that religion is not entirely deviance. Why
might that be so? Or perhaps, if there were a point to differentiate
Buddhism from Aum, where would we find that? One might say that
Buddhism's greatest strength is that it has been tested and forged in its
long history. All those we call world religions are the crystallizations
of the wisdom of humankind, which have passed such trials of history. Because of this, while they deviate from the world of *ningen*, they
simultaneously have a part that can be reduced to the human world,
and they preserve that tensional, back and forth relation. Of course, if
a religion loses its transgressive energy and is absorbed into the world
of *ningen*, it becomes a mere husk of religion. It is because of this transgressive energy alone that religion can have a strength uncontainable
by the domain of the human.

Therefore, religion takes a form that is adapted to the circumstances within its respective society. It has its legs planted in two
worlds: while conforming to the domain of *ningen*, it transgresses it.
This is exactly where the tensional relationship between religion and

---

8. 『バガヴァッド・ギーター』 [Bhagavad Gītā], trans. by Uemura Katsuhiko 上村勝彦
(Tokyo: Iwanami Bunko, 1992), ch. 21.32. See Eknath Easwaran, trans., *The Bhagavad
Gita* (Tomales, CA: Nilgiri Press, 2007).

ethics comes about. While religion often makes compromises with ethics; nevertheless, it tries to overcome it. Amidst this dialectic, religion encounters the other. While one may try to reduce the other to *ningen*'s world of meaning, one needs to confront an irreducible other. This is the problem of trans-ethics.

THE POTENTIAL AND LIMITS OF RELIGIOUS ETHICS

Despite the trans-ethical nature of religion, it is still possible to a certain extent to have a religious ethics. As I have discussed in Chapter 8, one possibility is a path like that of Socially Engaged Buddhism. However, that is merely within the scope of the domain of *ningen*, and it does not possess universality that transcends that domain—it is not absolute.

From a Japanese perspective, when one speaks of religious ethics, one cannot help but think about the various activities coming from the Christianity of Europe and America. Certainly, Christianity has had very vibrant social action, and there is much to learn there. However, not everything can be imported, and there are cases that depend on ideas peculiar to Christianity. Because of this, one cannot simply transplant this to Japanese soil. Christianity is no more than a reference, and we Japanese need to search for a path unique to Buddhism, or unique to Japan.

Previously, I had a discussion with someone who was active in Christian hospice about the views of life and death in Christianity and Buddhism. In the Christian conception, when a person dies, he or she goes to heaven. Heaven is a separate world with no direct relationship with this world. As a result, the consciousness of death as a total departure from this world is strong. Not to mention, even for people who do not have much faith, there is a powerful sense of dread that death is a return to nothingness. In this situation, in order to alleviate this fear and strengthen faith, hospice and the like are seen as very necessary.

However, because Buddhism has the concept of transmigration, the consciousness that death brings about a separation from this world is weak. Also, in Japan, we have the tradition of ancestor worship, and there is this conception that the dead watch over the living as gods or spirits. And so in this respect, it is not easy to feel that death results in an absolute separation from this world.

For sure, old faiths are in the process of changing, and we cannot be sure that people today still believe in such visions of the afterlife. However, there is a psychological structure within that does not change all that much, and it is unlikely that the Japanese conception will change over to a western one of heaven or nothingness. If this is so, then western hospice will not necessarily work in Japan, and may not be as necessary. We have to give sufficient consideration to such backgrounds. Talking about universal ethics is impracticable theory. As no more than a problem of *ningen*, we need to think while reflecting sufficiently on the way of being of our respective societies.

13

Religion Overcomes Ethics

The world of ethics that comes into being in the "between-ness of persons" is not a perfectly self-contained system. There are elements that spill out of it, and it is in these that the sphere of religion comes to light. In Buddhism, the notion that religion transcends the secular may seem to have begun with Śākyamuni's departure from householder life, thus becoming a core principle of Buddhism. But actually, the direct assertion that Buddhism transcends ethics is not that old—in Japan, it began in the Meiji period (1868–1912). Contrary to that, in the Edo period, Buddhism actively taught secular ethics, in response to the criticism from Confucians that Buddhism ignores ethics.

It was the True Pure Land Ōtani sect reformer, the renowned Kiyozawa Manshi (1863–1903), who exhaustively pursued the problems of religion and ethics and preached their mutual opposition. Kiyozawa studied philosophy at Tokyo University and began as a young religious philosopher. But later, as a religious sect reformer with his eyes fixed on his impending death by tuberculosis, he probed deeply into the essence of faith. In particular, the spiritualism (*seishin-shugi*) movement he propagated with his disciples in his last years was an important step for the establishment of modern religion in Japan. Kiyozawa received both considerable praise and censure within his sect. He did not receive sufficient consideration and assessment from outside his sect. But recently, Iwanami Shoten has released a new edition of his collected works, and more and more opportunities are arising to give him due attention.

In order to understand Kiyozawa's movement, it is necessary to know the spiritual conditions of society during his time. In 1889, the Meiji Constitution was promulgated, and Japan settled into its shape as a modern state. However, this also established a state polity that absolutized the emperor. Furthermore, in the following year, the government enacted the Imperial Rescript on Education, and that system was enforced upon the populace in the form of an established national morality enacted via school education. It was truly an era of morality.

Representing the conformist side of that day was the philosopher Inoue Tetsujirō. When the Christian Uchimura Kanzō got embroiled in this case of disrespecting the Imperial Rescript on Education, Inoue Tetsujirō took the chance to stir up the debate on "the collision of education and religion" and set out to denounce Christianity (1892–93). Here, "religion" concretely referred to Christianity, and "education" referred to the morals of the Imperial Rescript on Education. But anyhow, here, for the first time, religion was directly problematized as being contradictory to ethics and morality. A universalism / egalitarianism like Christianity could not fit within the present social order's state morality.

Although it was Christianity that received the brunt of the attack, the transcendence of the secular by *any* religion was put to question. It was thus a concern for Buddhism as well. However, the Buddhists back then were naïve on this point, and they sided with Inoue, seeing it as no more than a good chance to denounce Christianity. It took a few years for the Buddhists to realize the severity of the problem. Kiyozawa was one of those who took it seriously. In 1900, Kiyozawa formed the Kōkōdō with his disciples, and in the next year, they published the journal *The Spiritual World*, and began the activities of the spiritualist movement. Only two years lapsed before Kiyozawa passed away, but his activities during that span would form one of the most fruitful points of Japan's modern religious history.

From infinite responsibility
to "irresponsibilism"

Kiyozawa preached that by contemplating deeply into one's *kokoro* (heart-mind, the spiritual) rather than on the external world, one can encounter the absolutely infinite being—Tathāgata (the one who has thus come/gone, Nyorai)—and one ought to act as Tathāgata bids. That is the religious ultimate.

In that case, what then is secular morality? According to Kiyozawa, secular morality exists in order to make us realize that morality is impossible. Everything in this world exists mutually related to each other. This is what Buddhism calls "dependent arising." Kiyozawa called this "the unity of all things." If this is true, we are responsible not only to those who are close at hand, but to everyone and everything in the world.

However, is it even possible to carry out one's responsibilities toward everything in the world? Can we really be accountable for what happens in the back-alleys of the other side of the world, even given the extent of globalization's progress? That is completely unfeasible for us finite beings. Not to mention the other side of the world—we cannot even be completely responsible for those nearest at hand. The only one capable of this is the absolute infinite being, Tathāgata. If so, then we ought not to cling to our finite selves, but rather should cast ourselves aside and entrust everything to Tathāgata. Tathāgata takes on everything.

In this way, the infinite responsibility wherein one needs to take on everything is ceded to Tathāgata in our encounter, and thus turns into irresponsibility. "Irresponsibility" may seem like a terrible thing, but Kiyozawa's disciples used the word "irresponsibilism" in a positive way.

But if one entrusts everything completely to the other power (*tariki*) of Tathāgata, how are we to deal with secular matters? On this point, Kiyozawa consistently takes an extremely radical stance. If there was an injured person by the roadside, should one care for this person, or just quietly pass this person by? In response to this question, Kiyozawa answered, "Infinite great compassion is manifest within one's mind. If it orders one to care for this person, one cares for this person. If it orders one to pass this person by, one passes this person by."[9]

Kiyozawa's position is remarkably consistent. He completely rejects secular ethics and morality. Kiyozawa says, "There are those who say that it is inexpedient to destroy morality just because one preaches religion. This is a difficult problem, but it cannot be helped in any way. If morality is that easy to destroy, then it may be well to let it meet its ruin."[10]

PROBLEMS IRREDUCIBLE TO SECULAR ETHICS AND MORALITY

Kiyozawa's clear assertion dealt a severe blow against the ideology of the omnipotence of state morality that held currency during his time. However, I would feel a bit anxious if people abided by his ideas wholesale. Even if one might believe in Tathāgata and entrust oneself to Tathāgata, will Tathāgata really teach us how to deal with every single little matter in our secular lives? Will the idea that Tathāgata shoulders all responsibility, whereas we are not responsible for anything, ever gain currency in this world?

If someone refutes me by saying that my words are caused by my lack of faith, I will be hard-pressed for a comeback. But the world is not made up entirely of devoutly faithful people. And worse yet, today presents us with countless ambiguous issues that need to be decided. Even if one entrusted oneself to Tathāgata's power, would one not need to take responsibility when facing the world at large, rather than just leaving it to Tathāgata? Such are the problems of the ethics of *ningen*.

9. Kiyozawa Manshi 清沢満之「精神主義と他力」[Spiritualism and Other-power].

10. Kiyozawa,「宗教的道徳（俗諦）と普通道徳の交渉」[Discussions of Religious Morality (Simplified Teaching) and Universal Morality].

Despite these problems, Kiyozawa's righteous stance—never ingratiating itself to the ethics and morals of this world—gives us much courage. It is not that religion ought to deal with all the problems in the secular world, just because ethics and morality are being put to question. But it is precisely because we advocate ethics and morality that it becomes dangerous if we forget that which originally eludes the grasp of ethics and morality. If ethics consists in the issues of inter-personal rules, then the bigger problems lie in the very space that is irreducible to ethics. Is it not *that* which we must seek out more deeply? Tathāgata, to whom Kiyozawa devoted himself to, can be encountered nowhere else but in this place, as the other that escapes our comprehension.

COMING TO TERMS WITH HUMAN EXISTENCE AS ORIGINALLY MEANINGLESS

In modern Pure Land teaching, the problem of religion and ethics was often argued in relation to the idea of the "salvation of evil persons" in the *Lamentations of Divergences*. This also became a big issue in Zen Buddhism. However, allow me to change my angle here, and introduce a Buddhist who pursued the theory of the negation of ethics to an extreme: the almost unheard-of thinker named Maida Shūichi (1906–1967).

Maida was a philosopher who studied under Nishida Kitarō at the Kyoto Imperial University. But he was also the disciple of Kiyozawa's best pupil, Akegarasu Haya. Maida worked as a middle school and normal school teacher at his hometown, Kanazawa. However, after the war (1946), he abruptly cast aside his occupation and family, and ran away. He began his religious activities in Nagano prefecture, amidst abject poverty, and supported only by a few fervent believers. He spent the rest of his life writing and on missionary work. Perhaps he was greatly affected by the sudden change of values in Japan after losing the war. Maida studied the Āgama sutras, Prince Shōtoku, Shinran, and Dōgen, and developed his own view of Buddhism.

In one of the books Maida published in his last years, *In the Clear Light of the Moon*,[11] he appended a commentary entitled "The Buddhist Standpoint of Everydayness" to a translation of the classic early Buddhist text, the *Sutta-Nipāta*. In this commentary, he writes that human existence is meaningless. It is the same as having climbed to the summit of Everest—that has no meaning whatsoever. Although life is originally meaningless, people try to give it meaning. It is there where the "ought," "I have to..." come about. However, such an ought is both tragic and comic. Throw that ought out! Without an ought, our ignorance disappears as well.

> It is natural that flowers in the meadow bloom beautifully. It is also natural for Truman to have the atomic bomb built, order it dropped on Hiroshima and Nagasaki, and declare that he feels no guilt... How did the Japanese military carry out those stupid atrocities in the Chinese continent and elsewhere? ... One cannot say that it was in order to learn of one's foolishness, and to never again repeat that foolishness, and thus be wise. It is the human being that is, as usual, eternally foolish.... It is the human being that is capable of both kindness and cruelty. Nature has made human beings in this way.

He was basically saying that if it is human nature to be foolish, then it cannot be helped.

Perhaps one might think that this is taking it too far. Given that people are questioning the war responsibility of Buddhists, these words risk being misunderstood. Although it takes a different route, it gets pretty close to the affirmation of how things presently are, as in the doctrine of *hongaku* and the theories of emptiness and non-duality. However, if one takes it as an antithesis to the discourse that immediately tries to resolve things within ethics and morality, then Maida can be seen as accurately expressing, in his own way, a part of religion.

11. Maida Shūichi 毎田周一『澄む月のひかりに』[In the clear light of the moon] (1964).

14

Religion's Recurring Compromises with Ethics

Both Kiyozawa Manshi and Maida Shūichi tried to separate religion from ethics to an extreme. Because of this, they showed that religion transcends secular ethics, and in some cases, may even oppose secular ethics. In contrast, of course there were also critiques against their approach.

In the first place, Kiyozawa's theory of transcending ethics kept in mind the "collision between education and religion" debate that Inoue Tetsujirō stirred up. Kiyozawa's was also a Buddhist response to that. According to Inoue,[12] Christianity was incompatible with the circumstances in Japan for the following reasons:

1. It does not take the state as central.
2. It does not emphasize loyalty and filial piety.
3. It emphasizes leaving this world, and makes light of this world.
4. Its notion of love for humankind is like Mozi's *fraternité*—a love without [proper] discrimination.

Looking at these reasons, one sees that all of them apply not only to Christianity but to Buddhism as well. Incidentally, Mozi's *fraternité*[13] refers to how Mozi sees all people as equal, and advocates loving without discrimination. In contrast, Confucianism argues that rules vary depending on the kind of human relationship: parent-child, sov-

---

12. Inoue Tetsujirō 井上哲次郎『教育ト宗教ノ衝突』[The collision of education and religion] (1893).

13. 兼愛.

ereign-subject, husband-wife, elder-younger sibling, etc. This was the core principle of feudal society.

If we consider the case of Buddhism, we see that first, the truth of Buddhism goes beyond the framework of the state. Of course, Buddhism has the ideal ruler of this world: the *cakravartin* (the divine king who turns the dharma-wheel). But the Buddha, who preaches religious truth, is higher than such a king. This principle is maintained in the southern transmission of Buddhism until today. Even in China, there was a debate surrounding *śramaṇas* not respecting the monarch. A *śramaṇa* (household-leaver, monastic) does not owe the secular king any reverence, and that principle was upheld across the six dynasties of China.

The second reason is almost identical to the fourth. In Buddhism, the notion equivalent to love is compassion (*karuṇā*), and it is directed to all sentient beings. It is therefore different from the secular morality of Confucianism, wherein rules differ depending on relationship. Not to mention feudal morality and the Imperial Rescript on Education—there is something in Buddhism that definitely does not fit with these.

The third reason pulls together all of the separate issues, and succinctly expresses the difference between religion and morality. In China, we already had the criticism that Buddhism rejects secular morality. From the morality of Confucianism that states that "my body, my hair, my skin, are all a gift from my father and mother," Buddhist actions that include shaving one's head, abandoning one's home, and becoming a monastic, can naturally be subjected to the criticism that these go against secular morality.

In this way, it makes sense how Buddhism would also be the target of criticism. However, despite that, Inoue's main target was Christianity, and most Buddhists of that day took Inoue's side and saw this as a perfect opportunity to attack Christianity. Inoue defended Buddhism, writing, "In Buddhism, there are teachings relating to the state and to loyalty and filial piety, and on this point is quite different from Christianity."[14]

HOW DID BUDDHISM HOLD ITS OWN
AGAINST SECULAR POWERS?

If one examines the history of Buddhism in Japan, Buddhism has a long record of the "spiritual protection of the state."[15] In the ancient period, Buddhism was imported as *state Buddhism*, and was policed via the Law on Monks and Nuns. But it is not that the Buddhist world was entirely under state control. In the medieval period, there was the saying that, "The monarch's laws and the Buddha's laws are mutually dependent," and the two were seen as the two wheels of a carriage. Just like the medieval Catholic Church in the west, medieval Buddhist temples had enough power to rival the state. Religions had great power, and their mystical force was enough to undermine the state. Because of this, neither the state nor Buddhism were to be trifled with. The pardon of the tyranny of priest soldiers had this sort of power politics in the background.

Because of this, young royalty and aristocrats who could not be installed into power in the secular world went to temples. Temples were also asylums for the defeated, criminals, the infirm, women, and other "weak" members of society. If the secular world was the "front," then the world of Buddhism was the "back" that supported it. Thus, the latter was extraterritorial, and the laws and ethics of the secular world did not apply there.

But at the same time, in order for the Buddhist world to deal with secular authorities as equals, the former had to also recognize the orders of the secular world and compromise with them. If they completely ignored or infringed upon secular ethics, then the order of the

14. Ibid., 125.
15. 鎮護国家.

religious world would fall as well. Just as the world in front cannot stand without the world behind it, the world behind cannot stand without the world in front. It is only in the tight intermingling of the two that a complete world order is possible.

COMPROMISES WITH SECULAR ETHICS

However, toward the end of the Warring States period (approx. 1467–1568), that extraterritoriality could no longer be maintained. As can be seen in Oda Nobunaga's razing of the temples at Mt. Hiei and Toyotomi Hideyoshi's control of Hongan-ji, secular powers overpowered the Buddhist world. Buddhism needed to regroup amidst such a situation. It was Suzuki Shōsan's (1579–1655) Buddhist vocational theory of work that was among those that opened new avenues for Buddhism in these dire times. Shōsan was originally a Mikawa samurai serving the Tokugawas, but when he was 42, he suddenly took tonsure and began rigorous training in Zen. Through this, he built his own view of Buddhism—a theory of the occupations as the deeds of a buddha—wherein carrying out one's secular duties was tantamount to the acts of a buddha. For instance, Shōsan writes:

> Agriculture is an act of a buddha.... While toiling in the bitter cold or intense heat, one should take one's farming tools, and, taking as one's own enemies the clumps and overgrowths of worldly desires, plow and gather, and farm, carrying out the duties one has set one's mind to.... In this way, in the hours of the day, one carries out the activity of Buddha. Farmers should not seek any other deeds of a buddha.[16]

When each social class—samurai, farmers, artisans, and merchants—carries out its own social function to the full, this is none other than the deeds of a buddha. Such deeds are not restricted to becoming a monk and engaging in spiritual cultivation. Giving one's all in one's secular occupation is part of the deeds of a buddha. In this

16. Suzuki Shōsan 鈴木正三『万民徳用』 [The use of virtue for all people].

way, Shōsan's theory established a Buddhist secular ethics, and he was received very well in the post-war period. It was as if he played the same role as Protestantism's secular ethics in the west, laying the foundations for modern society.

But on the other hand, there is also a criticism against Shōsan's Buddhist vocational theory of work—that it was at the frontline of the Tokugawa shogunate's policy to fix social classes and it helped create the feudal order. There is more: Shōsan advocated using Buddhism to govern the masses, which was realized with the establishment of the temple registry system. Should religion deeply involve itself in the problems of secular ethics, or not? This is a tricky question.

After this, Buddhists like Hakuin and Jiun preached social ethics on the basis of Buddhism. Furthermore, it was in the Edo period that monks often abandoned austere practices, took wives and had children, and quickly secularized. However, despite that, Buddhism in the Edo period did not entirely secularize. Rather, Buddhism formed a domain separate from the secular world, and temples continued to be regarded as sacred grounds.

With the coming of modernity, this secularization would be completed, at least institutionally. Nevertheless, even today, it has yet to be completely secularized. On the one hand, there are waves of secularization that have washed over Buddhism, but on the other hand, you have theories, like Kiyozawa's, that advocate the transcendence beyond secular ethics. This is the conflict that occurs *because* Buddhism secularizes, and thus people are driven to ask, conversely, how to establish the position of Buddhism as a religion within that secular order.

In the path leading to the present, many Buddhist groups went through many hardships and made compromises with secular ethics. In wartime, they supported state policies towards the war. In peacetime, they were pacifists. In a time that calls for environmental protection, they preach ecological mindedness. In this way, Buddhist groups have tended to float along with the tides of secular ethics. But they did not totally adhere to secular ethics; they also showed their own tenacity. This tenacity can be called the contemporary form of the idea of the mutual dependence between the monarch's laws and the Buddha's laws, which has been refined ever since the medieval period.

TRANSGRESSION OF SECULAR ETHICS AS AUTHENTIC BUDDHISM?

There is another separate trend in the relationship between Buddhism and ethics. In this case, we do not merely see a transcendence of ethics, but a violation of ethics, that results in evil acts. For example, in the group of Hōnen, who preached the exclusive devotion to *nenbutsu* (intoning one's dependence on Amitābha) in the early Kamakura period, there were those who would assert that "If you fear sin and avoid evil, then you are a person who does not depend on Buddha."[17] This is the theory of unobstructed creation of evil, and such an assertion is also present in Shinran's school. The theory of the salvation of evil persons is part of this tradition.

These theories refer to sexual relations and meat-eating—Buddhist "evils" but not necessarily transgressions against secular ethics. But in a period wherein religious morality and secular ethics overlapped, this sort of assertion was in itself considered to be a crime that threatened the social order. In the latter part of the *Kōfuku-ji Petition*, which detailed complaints against Hōnen's school, it argued against "the error of bringing chaos to the country," strongly criticizing the destruction of the order of the mutual dependence of the monarch's and the Buddha's laws (wherein the two kinds of laws are two faces of the same coin). It argued that the intervention and even the oppression by secular authorities was something that could not be prevented. Hōnen's school actually ended up being persecuted due to its followers "disturbing the peace."

17. See 『興福寺奏状』 [*Kōfuku-ji petition*].

It seems natural for us to think that this attitude of disrupting social order ought to be subject to criticism. Well, to the contrary, scholars in the modern period unexpectedly think quite highly of this "anti-authoritarian" attitude. They often suggest that it is this theory of the mutual dependence of the laws of the monarch and the Buddha that is itself a form of collusion between religious and secular powers. Thus it was Hōnen's group, by having tried to formulate an egalitarian view of the salvation of people, which displayed the original form of Buddhism.

In this way, we see that there are various complications in the relationship between Buddhism and secular ethics, and there is no single answer as to how to evaluate that. One cannot be naïve and say which one is right and which is wrong. The only thing we can clearly say is that ethics is a problem restricted to the dimension of *ningen*, and it is in the transcendence of that wherein the greater task of religion lies. When one loses sight of that, even a great teaching ceases to be religious at all.

15

The Specter of the Other

Religion deviates from the domain of *ningen*, the "between-ness of persons," and engages the incomprehensible other. In the domain of *ningen*, people can mutually understand each other via various roles. But because of its deviation from such, religion goes beyond ordinary ethics. Yet despite this, at the base of the comprehensible domain of *ningen*, one is always compelled to relate with the unintelligible other. Let us examine the concrete manifestation of this by considering *The Lotus Sutra*.

In Japan, we use the 28 chapters of the *Myōhōrenge kyō*, based on the Kumārajīva translation, as *The Lotus Sutra*. The interpretation of this text is most commonly made via that of the Tendai school, and it divides *The Lotus Sutra* into two parts. The first half is called the *shakumon*, the gate of traces, where Buddha is described as a spatiotemporally restricted being, including up to "Chapter XIV. Ease in Practice."[18] The second half is called the *honmon* or main gate, and goes from "Chapter XV. Bodhisattvas Emerging from the Earth" onward. The gate of traces is centered around "Chapter II. Skillful Means," which takes up "explaining the three to reveal the one," which means bringing the three paths of Theravāda and Mahāyāna (*śrāvaka*, *pratyekabuddha*, and bodhisattva) back to the one single path of Buddhahood (the Buddha vehicle, S. *Ekayāna*). The main gate is centered around "Chap-

---

18. [We are using the titles from the BDK English Tripiṭaka Series. See Kubo Tsugunari, Yuyama Akira, trans., *The Lotus Sutra*, Revised 2nd Ed. (Berkeley: Bukkyō Dendō Kyōkai and Numata Center for Buddhist Translation and Research, 2007).]

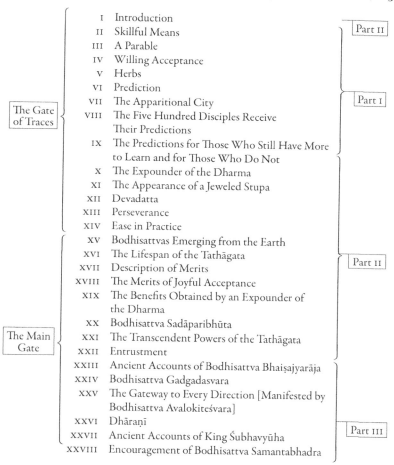

Figure 1. The Structure of *The Lotus Sutra*

ter XVI. The Lifespan of the Tathāgata," which takes up "explaining the near to reveal the far,"[19] which means taking the historical Buddha who awakened to enlightenment at the Bodh Gaya (thus called Gayajōdō no Shaka, the Buddha who Attained the Way at Bodh Gaya), as in the gate of traces, as an expedient means (a provisional means taken on to

19. 開近顕遠.

save sentient beings). With this approach, the main gate expresses "the Buddha as eternal truth" (Kuon Jitsujō no Shaka, the Buddha Truly Attained in the Distant Past), who transcends the historical Buddha.

Incidentally, modern research has looked into the development of *The Lotus Sutra*, and has divided it into three. The first part is from "Chapter II. Skillful Means" until "Chapter IX. The Predictions for Those Who Still Have More to Learn and for Those Who Do Not." The second is from "Chapter X. The Expounder of the Dharma" to "Chapter XXII. Entrustment," in addition to the introductory chapter. And the third part is from "Chapter XXIII. Ancient Accounts of Bodhisattva Bhaiṣajyarāja" onward. The third part includes the faith in various bodhisattvas, and was probably incorporated much later. Between the first and the second parts, it is probably the first that was written earlier. In recent years, a different theory, which argues that all 27 chapters (excluding the one on Devadatta) were written at around the same time, is gaining some legitimacy. But even this theory demarcates clearly between the first and second parts.

Recent interpretations argue that *The Lotus Sutra* can be read consistently as a bodhisattva philosophy. As the first part is fundamentally the same as the gate of traces, it is centered around the chapter on "Skillful Means" and the idea of "explaining the three to reveal the one." That "one" is the way of the Buddha, wherein anyone can attain Buddhahood. But as in the present we are not yet buddhas but rather in a preparatory stage, we can be called bodhisattvas. That can be rephrased as the formula: "All sentient beings are bodhisattvas."[20]

To put it simply, the "three" suggests that since we by no means possess the ability to become buddhas, we should be content with the most reachable state we can attain. In contrast, the standpoint of the "one" suggests that although we may get caught up in the idea that we

20. See Kariya Sadahiko 苅谷定彦『法華経：仏乗の思想』[The *Lotus Sūtra*: The theory of the Buddhist vehicles] (Japan: Tōhō Shuppan, 1983).

do not have the ability to become buddhas, that is not the case at all—everyone possesses that ability.

No sentient being can exist without the other

The second half of *The Lotus Sutra* discusses the problems of the practices of bodhisattvas after Buddha's passing. I will discuss the notion of the Buddha as one of the dead in Part III of this book (Chapter 21). So here, allow me to initially examine the first half of *The Lotus Sutra* in more detail. I have already taken up the idea of the bodhisattva (Chapters 4 and 5), and as I mentioned there, bodhisattvas in Mahāyāna, in principle, exist with others. But the mere fact that they focus on "benefitting others" does not guarantee a sense of ethicality toward others. The first half of *The Lotus Sutra* probes deeply into this aspect of bodhisattvas.

The notion of "explaining the three to reveal the one" in the chapter "Skillful Means" clearly argues that *śrāvakas* and *pratyekabuddhas*—previously considered no more than paths of the "small vehicle"—are in truth none other than bodhisattvas (of the "great vehicle"), and will attain Buddhahood at some point. But that interpretation alone is quite abstract. By my own interpretation, it means that while the disciples of the Buddha had thought that they did not need the other, and that they could exist alone and self-sufficient, they realized that they are beings that require the other. "All sentient beings are bodhisattvas" means that "no sentient being can exist without the other."

Perhaps someone might say that this idea—that nobody can exist without cooperating with others—is quite matter of fact. But actually, it is a serious problem as to whether or not this "matter of fact" can stand as a core principle. As I have mentioned, early Buddhism did not make this into a core principle. And as soon as Mahāyāna Buddhism turned it into a core principle, things got very complicated, and ethics began to get pretty fuzzy.

Amidst these concerns, the notion of the other presented in *The Lotus Sutra* is by no means simplistic. It is definitely *not* the other people we can mutually communicate in our everyday lives with a certain ease—not the "inter-personal" other. Rather, it is an unintelligible other, symbolized by the Buddha, that abruptly manifests in a place transcending the inter-personal.

This is discussed in detail in "Chapter III. A Parable" and onward, which continue from "Skillful Means." This is called the assurance of future enlightenment for *śrāvakas*, wherein it is elucidated by the Buddha that the *śrāvakas* of Hīnayāna (the Buddha's disciples) are actually bodhisattvas, and he prophecies (S. *vyākaraṇa*) that after a long period of time, they will eventually become buddhas. What might this mean?

ŚĀKYAMUNI REPRESENTS THE OTHER

In "A Parable," the Buddha prophesies Śāriputra's attainment of Buddhahood. (Śāriputra was part of the dialogue in "Skillful Means.") It is prophesied that in a future life, after an infinitely long amount of time, Śāriputra would attain Buddhahood and become the Tathāgata Padmaprabha. However, why is it that Śāriputra, thought to be a *śrāvaka* incapable of Buddhahood, can become a buddha? The answer lies in the causes and conditions of the past. We find out here that Śākyamuni had previously taught Śāriputra in the presence of 200 million buddhas. The relationship with Śākyamuni did not arise abruptly in the present—but Śāriputra could not recall this any longer.

This sort of a relationship with the other can no longer be fully grasped within the ethics of the inter-personal that arises as mutual role relations in the present. In "the causes and conditions of previous lives," we see that "previous lives" are not meant in the ordinary sense, but in the continuing causes and conditions continuing from the almost infinite past. The relationship with the other needs to be considered from the point of view of the temporality of the infinitely long stretch of the past and the future. Furthermore, the present and the future are both shaped by the past, and the past is given in the weightiest manner. But of course, this past is not the linear temporal past in the physical sense, but rather the past that dwells in the furthest depths within us. Perhaps one could say that it is buried in our genes.

That past is long forgotten. Perhaps people want to forget this troublesome relationship with the other as quickly as possible. And yet in spite of that, even if we may seem to be oblivious on the surface, the other still haunts us and ceaselessly awakens memories that ought to have been completely forgotten. To rouse these memories, retrieve them, and make space for them is what it means to become a bodhisattva.

Here, Śākyamuni appears as a representative of the other. I think the relationship between Śākyamuni and Śāriputra can be understood by replacing it with the deep relationship between myself and another—parent-child, husband-wife, any relationship will do. For sure it is not all rosy with this relationship. No matter how hard I try to figure out why I am bound to this person with an unbreakable bond, I cannot find a clear-cut answer. It is not just love—sometimes you hate someone so much you could kill them. If you could divorce them and be done with it, then that is that. But even if you actually killed this person, although it may seem like you have done away with this person's existence entirely, in actuality, you remain bound, from the beginning, in this relationship with the other—that never disappears, that ceaselessly haunts, that never leaves.

This message of *The Lotus Sutra* is often overlooked. People highlight only the idea that "anyone can become a buddha." The causes and conditions of the past, found in the "Skillful Means" chapter, are not explained.

Furthermore, in "A Parable," which takes up the destined bond between Śākyamuni and Śāriputra, we also find the famous metaphor of the burning house of the triple world. In this metaphor, a wealthy man tries to save his children from a burning house through skillful means. He promises to give his children their favorites—a sheep carriage, a deer carriage, and an ox carriage. But as soon as they get to a safe place, he gives them an even grander large carriage, driven by a large white ox. It shows that the three vehicles are skillful means, and the single Buddha vehicle alone is the truth. However, a careful reader will notice that this story presupposes the unbreakable mutual relationship between parent and child, which is embedded within the metaphor.

THE RELATIONSHIP WITH THE OTHER THAT EXTENDS FROM THE INFINITE PAST TO THE INFINITE FUTURE

So what then happens to the idea of attaining Buddhahood? If the destined connection between Śākyamuni and Śāriputra begins in the infinite past, then attaining Buddhahood gets pushed forward into the unthinkably distant infinite future—an unreachable dimension. However, if we see the infinite past as interwoven within the present, then the infinite future is, in some way, already realized within the present. Bodhisattvas and buddhas are not that far apart. Śākyamuni, so long as he continues to relate with sentient beings throughout eternity, is himself fully a bodhisattva.

Here, the most important thing is that the ground for a bodhisattva to be a bodhisattva is to engage the other to the very end. It is not some substantive foundation like Buddha-nature or *Tathāgatagarbha*. *The Lotus Sutra*'s theory that "all sentient beings are bodhisattvas" is often linked to the philosophy of "all sentient beings have Buddha-nature (*tathāgatagarbha*)," found in *Tathāgatagarbha* / Buddha-nature theories. But really, there is a big gap between the two. *Tathāgatagarbha* / Buddha-nature is immanent within the self, and it does not need the relationship with the other. The bodhisattva in *The Lotus Sutra* is the opposite of that. The foundation of being a bodhisattva is not within the self, but is within the engagement with the other.

Perhaps it may seem unreasonable to try to understand the entirety of the theory of the bodhisattva in *The Lotus Sutra* from the point of view of the relationship with the other from the past to the future. But I assure you, it is not. In "Chapter VII. The Apparitional City," Buddha explains his relationship with the secular world through the causes and conditions connecting him to Mahâbhijñā-jñānâbhibhū-Buddha. This Buddha preached *The Lotus Sutra* in an infinitely distant past, and then passed away. But of his 16 princes, the 16th was Śākyamuni, and while the other princes were sent to teach in other worlds, Śākyamuni taught in our world (the Sahā world). Because of this, Śākyamuni said, "Because I have taught the highest enlightenment (of Buddha) to these people who now dwell in the state of being a *śrāvaka*, these people will, through my teaching, eventually enter the enlightenment of the Buddha."

Reading it in this way, it becomes clear that this scripture, *The Lotus Sutra*, is by no means just some inspirational text. What we see here is Buddha as the other, who pursues us endlessly, who shadows us, no matter how much we might despise it. The bond with the other is a space of raw conflict that cannot be reduced to inter-personal ethics as mere role-relations. Because it is a relationship that extends from the infinite past to the infinite future, there is no escaping it. If so, then we have no choice but to recognize that, take it up, and encounter the other face-to-face. But how can one confront the other that transgresses the order of *ningen*? This is a problem insoluble by ethics—a trans-ethical problem.

16

The Labyrinth of the Other: *Han* and *Ma*

When we wipe away the rules of *ningen*, the other shows itself in all its strangeness. There is no trouble so long as our mutual roles are clear and we understand how to respond to each other. But in the face of the sudden appearance of the incomprehensible visage of the other, we are reduced to bewilderment. Sometimes, the tangle of our emotions remains inexpressible through the words of *ningen*, and they clump up and explode in the most unexpected ways. Sometimes a child who seemed to have no troubles suddenly snaps, and to everyone's surprise gets into all sorts of disciplinary trouble. In the same way, complicated, anarchic sentiments blow up between ethnic groups and states. The problems of today are so complex that we cannot hope to solve them with the religions and ethical systems of the past.

More than in Buddhism, these sorts of problems are being seriously discussed in Christian theology. Since Christianity originally developed in the west, a west-centric (or Occidentalist, in the non-academic sense) way of thinking was once predominant. But since the birth of liberation theology, new theologies have developed which are based on areas other than the "west," and which take the standpoint of oppressed people as their points of departure. One example of this is Andrew Park's. He is a Protestant theologian of Korean descent, and his theology is that of *han* (resentment).[21]

21. [*Han* is the Korean pronunciation. Park translates it as "the shame felt by victims." From the context of Sueki's usage, it translates more elegantly to "resentment," sans the

According to Park, prior theologies have focused on human sin as the greatest issue, and have presupposed that through faith, we receive God's forgiveness. However, this is the logic of the aggressor, the strong, the oppressor. For although their sins may be forgiven, the suffering of the victims, the weak, the oppressed, remains unsettled.

In such a view, sin and forgiveness develop as a closed relationship between God and oppressors (the strong), from which victims (the weak) are excluded. In this setup, the negative feelings that pile up within the victims can be called *han*. In Japanese, *han* is closer to the word *onnen* (a grudge). But the Korean word, bearing the long history of suffering oppression, is much more to the point. Park's parents were born in Korea and suffered during the colonial period (under Japanese rule), and after Korea's independence, the north and south split and went to war, and they scrambled out, eventually escaping to the United States, where they died in a traffic accident. In this way, Park himself truly lived smack in the middle of *han*, beginning with the experiences of his parents.

According to Park, the sins of aggressors are, more than against God, against their victims. Just as the weak are wounded and come to bear this *han*, God too suffers and bears this *han*. Because of this, there is no way for oppressors to be forgiven, without trying to be freed from the *han* of the oppressed and to construct a world without *han*. It is the weak who first need to be saved, not the strong.

Park's theology of *han* is receiving attention for having provided a completely different approach to religion and ethics by speaking from the standpoint of the victims and the weak. *Han* is not just a Christian problem, but can be found everywhere in the world, both in the

___

negative nuance of "*ressentiment*" found in Nietzsche, Scheler, or psychoanalysis. Other translations of the character include "regret," "bearing a grudge," and "hate." I shall leave it as *han* for the most part.]

Andrew Park, *The Wounded Heart of God* (Nashville: Abingdon Press, 1993). See also, Morimoto Anri 森本あんり『アジア神学講義』[Lectures on Asian theology] (Tokyo: Sōbunsha, 2004).

religious and areligious spheres. Even more so, religion itself can harm others and can be the very thing that drives others into bearing *han*. Because of this, these issues cannot be resolved by the internal reflection of one religion alone. Park himself recognizes that *han* will be a central issue for interreligious dialogue. Is one's religion truly able to take the standpoint of the victims and the weak? And beyond mere talk, what are we actually doing to accomplish this? These are matters that deserve close scrutiny.

THE COMPLEX AGGRESSOR-VICTIM RELATIONSHIP

Buddhism often preaches letting go of hate. It is written in the *Dhammapada*: "Hatred is never appeased by hatred in this world." But *han* cannot be cast aside so easily. It is putting the cart before the horse to expect victims to cast away their *han* without even questioning the responsibility of aggressors.

So if aggressors acknowledged their sins at once, would that gradually erase the *han* of the victims? That is too optimistic. In the first place, there is no short supply of cases wherein the strong are not conscious at all of the fact that they have done wrong.

While the weak can be deeply wounded by the least of utterances, the strong who spit out these words do not necessarily realize that they have hurt the other. In the case of bullying, it can be such a severe problem for the bullied that he or she might want to trade his or her life for another's. But for the bullies, it is just a little fun. For a small country, something might be an unforgivable incursion, but for the invading, powerful state, it may be no more than an attempt to be just, or even to help out a developing nation. In this way, rather than *han* being alleviated, it is aggravated and made worse.

Furthermore, as Park himself recognizes, contemporary society is set up in such a complex way that it is not always clear who the aggressor is and who the victim is. A youth who commits a crime might also be a victim, when it comes to his or her problems at home or in school.

If a state that has suffered from a terrorist attack exacts retribution, this time around, it might become an aggressor that is responsible for the murder of innocents. The aggressor becomes the victim, the victim turns into the aggressor. Each time, *han* grows deeper, and the way to resolution grows ever distant. What do we do then?

Of course, there are no quick fixes. Park argues that the cause of *han* is mainly found in the social factors like global capitalist economics, patriarchy, and racial, ethnic, and cultural discrimination. By putting an end to these, *han* is resolved as well. These social problems are certainly crucial, and it would be a grievous error to turn a blind eye to the contradictions and injustice lurking within the very structure of society.

However, is it not too optimistic to think that everything can be fixed this way? We need to also recognize issues that cannot be reduced to social factors.

THE DEMON WITHIN

Kamata Tōji did not merely take the Aum Shinrikyō and the Sakaki Bara incident as problems outside himself, but rather, he considered them deeply as his own problems. He tried to grasp that which drove Asahara Shōkō and the boy Sakaki Bara to those deviant acts, as "the demonic" (*ma*).[22] Calling it "the demonic" might seem quite broad and vague, but it seems to be the best name for that something in the depths of one's existence that rational intelligence cannot keep up with. So we have little choice but to refer to this as "the demonic" (or "devils" [*akuma*] or "apparitions" [*mabutsu*]). If we consider this together with *han*, then we can schematize it as follows: It is the demonic, *ma*, that drives us to commit sin, and this awakens the *han* in others.

22. Kamata Tōji 鎌田東二 『呪殺・魔境論』 [A theory of death curses and haunting] (Tokyo: Shūeisha, 2004).

Saying someone was driven by "the demonic" may make it seem as if society or the persons themselves have no responsibility in the matter. But that is not the point. To put it broadly, the totality of the social order always becomes a problem, and the persons involved always have to take responsibility for wrongs committed. However, despite that, sometimes there is just something lurking within us that we cannot seem to control. The youth, Sakaki Bara, described this saying:

> Within the isolation cell of my mind and heart (*kokoro*)... standing deathly still like a ghost, what the hell is it looking at, this apparition, staring into the void? I couldn't get the faintest clue, even if I tried.[23]

Here he suggests that there is a "demon" lurking within him that not even he can fathom.

It is not just Sakaki Bara and Asahara Shōkō. In the hearts of the leaders of powerful states who believe that it is just to murder even innocent civilians, they must have the demonic dwelling within them as well. And that is not just for other people—we ourselves flounder about in the same way, in our banal everyday lives. Demons showed themselves before Jesus and Śākyamuni, and tried to impede their enlightenment and activities. While Jesus and Śākyamuni were able to powerfully banish these demons, that is not something ordinary folk can do. The demonic lurks within my own heart, weakening my will, driving me to do things against my own volition. Or perhaps it twists my very will. This is the other within me. The other is not merely someone outside.

Easy to enter the buddha-world, hard to enter hell

The rationalism of modernity has fallen into oblivion about the dead and has forgotten the fear of the demonic. There is this false

23. 手記「懲役13年」[Notes: "Thirteen years of penal servitude"].

security that people can judge rightly via reason and govern themselves through the power of the will, and this security has turned into smugness. But who can say if what you think is a good act in accordance with your will is not actually a demonic act that wounds others? How many people can really resist the temptations of the demonic? "If you can't beat 'em, join 'em." "Best to play it safe." Even in international relations, when one powerful state does something, most other states simply follow suit, no matter how twisted the powerful state's actions might be.

And of course, there are those who fall into despair with the realization that one cannot do good by one's own will. This is why the theory of the salvation of evil persons in the *Lamentations of Divergences* became so famous in modern Japan. But in this case, it is just as Park warned—the wounded other is forgotten, and the self that could not help but do evil is saved, through that evil, by Amitābha. It is a salvation of the aggressor alone. To put it harshly, that could be no more than a transaction within the collusion of Amitābha and the demonic. When Kiyozawa Manshi's disciples espoused the *akunin shōki setsu*, sure enough the more socially-oriented Buddhists criticized it as being against social ethics.

How do we ameliorate and settle *han* and *ma*, hatred and the demonic? To a certain extent, this can be discussed within the ambit of the ethics of *ningen*. I do not doubt the importance of this ethical approach. But nevertheless, the demonic is deeply rooted within our hearts and gives rise to *han*, and at any moment, *han* can call forth more *ma* and more *han*.

To begin with, if the demonic leads us to murder (be it of one person or *en masse*), is there any way to alleviate the *han* of the dead? Later on, we will discuss the most difficult issue—war and the dead (Chapter 24).

The task of trans-ethics is not to come up with mystic measures to solve these problems. Rather, it pushes us to stand, unflinching, before the relationship with the other (including myself as an other) that interweaves the demonic and *han*, and reconsider it, this time with a recovered sense of dread. In the beloved words of Kawabata Yasunari, "It is easy to enter the Buddha-world, but hard to enter hell." This expresses the above quite perfectly.[24]

24. These are said to be Ikkyū Sōjun 一休宗純's words, but they can actually be found in the records of his contemporary, Sekkō Sōshin 雪江宗深 (1408–1486).

17

Love is Also Deviant

What drives us to break out of the framework of the rules of *ningen* and do harm to the other is "the demonic." Through the pain caused, *han* is born. However, there are different ways of relating with the other that are possible, and one example is the mode of relating we call "love."

Love has various types, two of which are eros and agape. Eros is modeled after sexual love, and where one seeks to become one with the other. Platonic philosophy sees this type of love as the foundational passion of philosophy, wherein one aspires for truth. In contrast, agape, in Christianity, is the love between human beings and God. But because there is a gap between the creator God, who is absolute, and created and finite human beings, agape requires the mediation of the intercessor, Jesus. However, even in the Platonic notion of "ideas" (seen without presupposing the Christian view of the divine absolute), love is an intense demand toward the other, where one desires to become one with or to possess the other.

In contrast, in Buddhism, love is also called *taṇhā* (thirst, J. *katsuai*, S. *tṛṣṇā*), where, just like a person ravenous with thirst, one loses all reason and desperately seeks for something to drink. These worldly desires that lead to attachment are the fundamental cause of people falling into delusion and becoming trapped within the suffering of transmigration. Buddhism also needs to negate *kāma*, a form of sexual desire emphasized in India. Sans its negative implications, this thirst is very similar to the western notion of love, given the intense yearning for its object.

Buddhism religiously affirms compassion (S. *karuṇā*), rather than thirst, as an attitude toward the other. However, pure compassion is impossible unless one is a perfected Buddha. It is not something anyone can do. Even if one tries to act compassionately, with the best of intentions, in at least some small aspect, one still ends up hurting the other or a third party. Also, it is impossible to be compassionate in a completely fair manner toward every single person. If my child and some stranger's child were both drowning, it would be perfectly natural for me to try to save my own kin first.

THE BARRIER BETWEEN SELF AND OTHER IS NOT DEFINITIVE

People try to connect with others. No matter how anti-social or self-isolating one may be, that too is because one fears being hurt by others, and is thus in a way, a strong call for the other. The bond between self and other seems to be such a precarious thing, but actually, the barrier between self and other is not something clear-cut.

When one tries to relate with others, sometimes one encloses oneself with the armor of a strong individuality, effectively walling off the self from the other. But sometimes, one does the opposite, dissolving all walls and melding into the other. Sometimes the other invades and enters the self. In these latter cases, the bounds of the "I" exceed the individual, and extend to the other that one unifies with. Or sometimes, one finds peace when the "I" is absorbed within the other and is lost.

A child is comforted by being one with his or her parents, and matures by internalizing their sense of values. On the side of the parents, they care for the child, feeling the child as if he or she were an inner presence. Of course, while this is the only way for child-rearing to be possible, there are times when this is not quite the often romanticized "beautiful love between parent and child." There are cases where parents and children try to dominate the object of their affection, and bind the other, trying to exclude all third parties from this closed relationship. And sometimes, when children mature, this very intimacy gives rise to intense conflict in both parent and child. The demonic lurks within love. Freud pointed out the Oedipal complex, wherein a sexual rivalry exists between a father and his son. He shook the world by clarifying how parent-child relationships are not as ideal as we make them to be.

These things also transform with changing historical and social conditions. In contemporary Japan, it is said that the conflict between father and son has weakened because of the collapse of the patriarchal, masculinist order, and the reduced need for children to achieve independence early on. But instead, it is the women (particularly housewives) who suffer more, amidst the shift toward nuclear families and low birth rates, where they are made to bear the responsibility for child-rearing. As a consequence, the unification between mother and child tends to be much stronger, and individuation becomes much more difficult. It is fundamentally because the rules of *ningen* within the family have become vague with the changing historical conditions, making parents more and more confused about how to treat their children, that child abuse has become such an unprecedentedly large social issue.

What we see here is that the issues surrounding love are not restricted merely to the domain of the heart and mind. The rules of *ningen* change with historical periods, and these are very much related to love. The changes of social structures—low birth-rates, an aging population—shape it greatly. Because of this, we need to consider these circumstances and consider how the rules of *ningen* ought to be positively transformed. There is no such thing as a universal morality of the family that applies to all periods in history.

On the other hand, it is certainly impossible to reduce all of our relations with the other to the rules of *ningen*. Just as love is a source of great joy, it is also a source of suffering. And worse, there are also times when we hurt the other, and this gives rise to the deepest resentment (*han*). That being said, we cannot live without love or attachment. It gushes out as an impulse we cannot do away with. Given that, we should not shut our eyes to love and attachment. The ambiguous relationship with the other takes these forms, whether we like it or not. Instead, should we not train our gaze upon it? Indeed, the saying that "worldly desires, as they are, are enlightenment" seems vulgar, dirty, nothing but the self-justification of egoistic desires, and completely out of joint with our times. However, there is something about the circumstances expressed by these words that retain their significance. It is this tempestuous love, which gives rise even to things like *han*, that is the most forthright relationship we have with the other.

THE MEDIATION OF THE DEAD MAKES THE RELATIONSHIP WITH THE OTHER POSSIBLE

The cellphone novel series *Deep Love* by Yoshi was a big hit amongst high school girls here in Japan. It probes into both the difficulties of love in this age, as well as how love might continue to be possible. The protagonist is a high school girl, Ayu, who lives with a gigolo, Kenji, while she herself makes money through "compensated dating" (schoolgirl prostitution). She was raped by her stepfather, and her mother committed suicide, so she always has a poker face on, and her favorite line is, "Tarukunai?" (Isn't it boring?)

She first opened up when she met an old lady, who lost her husband in a suicide squad and her little sister to an air raid, all on the same day. Through the death of this old woman, Ayu comes to know Yoshiyuki, who has a heart problem. Ayu, falling in love for the first time, yet needing to make the money for Yoshiyuki's surgery, gets thrown back into prostitution and catches AIDS, from which she slowly wastes away. Parts two and three unfold in this hopeless way, with the dying Ayu, Yoshiyuki who stays connected to her, and her friend Reina. A cruel fate continues to lash against the three, pushing them deeper into darkness.

Here, "sex" is separated from "love." Sex becomes mundane and perfunctory, and loses its original character as a relationship with the other. In contrast, Ayu and Yoshiyuki almost never touch, but still Ayu falls in love for the first time. She sacrifices her own body in order to make the money for Yoshiyuki's surgery. Is that "love?" Ayu's feelings are very one-sided, as far as love goes, and there is a lack of mutuality. As to the small sum she saves from prostitution, she gives it to Yoshiyuki's alcoholic father, only to have it wasted on drink.

Despite all this, it is in Ayu's encounter with Yoshiyuki that she first feels this intense sense of lack and desire. For the first time, she regains the other that had been lost by the commodification of sex. Prostitution is receiving money in compensation for sex, granted to sate a man's desires, and is no more than an exchange within the framework of *ningen*. But in meeting Yoshiyuki, the rules of *ningen* fall apart.

It is not for the sake of money or desire. But for some reason I do not understand, the other moves me, and drives me to acts that get me nothing in return. It is this irrational shock of the other that constitutes its otherness, its *alterity*. It is here where Ayu first experiences the other. Does it really matter if we call it "love," or if we call it by another name? When I call to the other, if the other answers—even if this answer may be from so far away—something irreducible to the domain of *ningen* is born.

A key point here is that in this encounter with the other/dead play a mediating role. It was the departed grandmother who brought Yoshiyuki and Ayu together. That old lady also lived that endless "postwar period" with her deceased husband and little sister, whom she lost during the war. The reason Ayu was first able to open herself to the old lady was perhaps partially because the old lady lived a life together with the dead, with those who cannot be reduced to the inter-human. And while at first glance, Ayu's death from AIDS and prostitution may seem meaningless, it continues to guide the lives of Yoshiyuki and Reina.

It is through the intercession of the dead that our relationship with the living other first becomes possible. As soon as we forget the departed, love between the living becomes impossible as well. I think this is not just a problem for these novels alone; it is a more general problem. Are the dead not the most important when thinking about the relationship with the living? I hope to take this up in Part III.

Let me get ahead of myself and point one thing out. In the ancient period, the call toward the sexual other was not all that different from the call of the dead. In the *Manyōshū*, the love songs called *sōmonka* (songs of romantic exchanges) are seen as part of the same set with elegies mourning the dead. Even more striking is that the poem by Empress Iwa no Hime, consort of Emperor Nintoku, placed at the start of the romantic exchange songs, can barely be distinguished from an elegy. For example, she writes,

> Long now are the days
> since my lord has gone away;
> as elder leaves meet,
> so shall I go and meet him
> and not wait an endless wait.[25]

This poem is usually seen as the call toward the sexual other, but it also makes sense to see it as the call to someone who is dead and never to return. Actually, the poet and scholar of Japanese Literature, Origuchi Shinobu, sees love (*koi*) as related to the invocation of the dead, that seeks to call back the souls of the departed. It is the dead who are the most important problem in the trans-ethical.[26]

Going back to *Deep Love*, allow me to add one thing. The prosecutor here is the self-satisfied grown-up face of moralism. Anyone can say that compensated dating is morally wrong. But who came up with the

25. [Translation from Edwin A. Cranston, *A Waka Anthology: The Gem-Glistening Cup* (Stanford: Stanford University Press, 1998), 51.]

26. Origuchi Shinobu 折口信夫「相聞歌概説」[Commentary on songs of romantic exchanges]『折口信夫全集』[Complete works of Origuchi Shinobu], vol. 9.

present framework of *ningen* wherein all that predominates are desires and money? Who is it who touts the justice of tormenting the weak with wars only the strong can win? Who insists that wagging one's tail at the strong is for the sake of "national interest?" How on earth are these "grown-ups" capable of teaching children morality and sensitivity? The ones who ought to reflect deeply on their wrongs are these grown-ups who have constructed this ossified order of *ningen*, which they do not even consider putting to question.

18

Nationalism and
Becoming One with the Other

People generally think that an individual existence that has a body and a mind is a "self," an "I." Certainly, in a commonsensical way, human society seems like a collection of such individual existences. However, as I have previously mentioned, the bounds of such a self are not as absolute as they seem. To put it very simply, when one drives a car, if one cannot estimate the dimensions of a car as extensions of one's own bodily dimensions, there would be no way to turn into a narrow road. To borrow Nishida Kitarō's parlance, this is a "pure experience" of the car and the self becoming one. To give another example, when I enter into a contract as an employee of a company, the "I" that entered this contract is not an "I" as an individual body and mind, but an "I" that represents the legal entity of a company.

Unlike the period when the family's labors were enough to give it a nearly self-sufficient existence, contemporary society comes together in a very complex way. Now, each person has so many different layers of human relations in which he or she is connected. When at work, the "I" is but an employee of a company; for instance, if a section chief makes a call, he or she cannot bring in family issues. However, the "I" after coming home is a spouse, a parent, and must concern oneself with things like the education of children.

This is not merely putting on roles. Rather, in accordance with each situation, the "I" assimilates into and is assimilated by the company or the family. If the products of one's company gain widespread acceptance, one feels happy even though one did not develop these products by oneself. If a child gets good grades, the parents feel proud of their child. These are not just about the spirit of dedication to one's company, or being a doting parent. In these instances, the "I" becomes one body with the company or with the family.

BECOMING ONE WITH THE NATION AND THE STATE

In this way, the self tries to transcend, and actually exceeds, the bounds of the body and the mind. Previously, I called this impulse to bridge the barrier between self and other, "love." Love is remarkably common and mundane, realized through dedication to one's company, devotion to one's family, etc. In Japanese, we call a car that one has gotten used to and, in a sense, become one with, as "my beloved car" (*aisha*). Through love, one is bound to the other, and a "thick relationship" with the other is born.

If becoming one with the other is brought to its widest, it would probably culminate in love for humankind. But in reality, such love is quite abstract, and so long as humankind is not attacked by aliens, such a love will probably never get past a mere "thin relationship."[27] In contrast, although it also seems abstract, what the individual quite easily unifies with is the nation or the state. Here, we have the problems of nationalism. Even though we may not be conscious about it on the surface, this unification influences us quite deeply, and in reality, it manifests even in everyday situations.

For example, in the Olympics, the activities of athletes from one's own country are broadcast widely, and people get quite interested. But the wins of foreign athletes do not get much airtime and much interest. When athletes like Ichirō and Matsui do well in the major leagues in the USA, Japanese people do not care much about whether the team won or lost, but are more interested in covering how the Japanese

27. For more on thick and thin relationships, see Chapter 24.

athletes played. When one's countryman is taken hostage in Iraq and killed, the whole country is up in arms. But if it is a foreigner, then it will not make the headlines. People think of this state of affairs as normal, and nobody seems to doubt that.

Of course this can be seen as an extension of local pride. While Tokyo newspapers play up the games of the Giants, Osaka newspapers focus on the Hanshin team. If it were just things like sports, there is no fault there. However, the state has the power to move the whole of its people, and as the subject of foreign relations, particularly the military and war, it can involve the entire nation.

Certainly, countries are just arbitrarily demarcated territories drawn on the globe, which then wage war on each other. One could say that states are "empty" (in the Buddhist sense) and that it is pointless to fuss over things like the state. Furthermore, others are of the opinion that the contemporary state is a product of modernity, and is something that ought to be negated. However, is it really feasible for an ordinary person to be a global citizen, without any single citizenship, acting freely regardless of where he or she goes? Perhaps it is for globe-trotting cosmopolitans. But if one's country is invaded by another and colonized, nobody is going to be able to take that sitting down.

When China was invaded by Japan, the Chinese Buddhists, after much bitter deliberation, decided to cooperate with the anti-Japanese resistance under the leadership of Taixu. Although Taixu was a household-leaver, a monk, he saw it necessary to protect the territory he lived in. He firmly refused collaboration with the Japanese and took the side of the anti-Japanese. While this might seem to be akin to the war cooperation of the Japanese Buddhists, the case of the Chinese is vastly different from the Japanese, who uncritically slid into cooperating with a war of aggression.

Nationalism and aggressive militarism

Nationalism often falls easily into the hands of political manipulation. Through education, citizens are brainwashed from an early age and lose their ability to see things critically. It is quite problematic. Both the invader and the invaded are driven by the nationalist sentiments of citizens, as we see clearly in Japan's war.

However, the original sense of nationalism need not be linked to wars of aggression. My reason for this is that if one suffers when one's country is invaded, then one should understand the pain of others who are invaded. For example, previously, when Korea was a Japanese colony, Japan carried out a policy of *sōshi kaimei*, whereby Koreans were forbidden from bearing their own names and were forced to take on Japanese names. In order for Japanese people to imagine how terrible that would be, all they need to do is imagine what it would feel like if their Japanese names were forbidden, and they were forced to take on the victor's names—Jack, Betty, etc.

The encounter with the other that is irreducible to the rules of *ningen* is not just for individual persons, but also holds true for countries and ethnic groups. In the latter case, one can only sympathize with the pain of the other if one understands one's own pain as a nationalist. A person who rejects nationalism and has no sense of pride in his or her own country could not possibly understand the *han* (resentment) of invaded peoples.

However, the strange thing is that nationalists often become the most vicious and aggressive militarists. Although they have pride in their own countries, they are completely numb to the pain felt by the other when he or she suffers invasion. To be blunt, people like these are not nationalists but plain egoists. It is no different from the twisted reasoning that if it would benefit one's own, then it would be good to intrude into another's house and commit burglary. People like that are a nuisance to their own countries, and ought to be strongly criticized and their stance rejected.

ŌKAWA SHŪMEI'S "MAHĀYĀNA" PAN-ASIANISM

However, in truth it is easy for nationalism to fall into the trap of aggressive militarism, even if one tries to be careful about it. Ōkawa Shūmei (1886–1957) is one of the representative thinkers of Japanese fascism, and is infamous as an ideologue for wars of aggression. However, Ōkawa first studied Indian philosophy, and because of that he knew the wretched state India was in under British colonial rule. And so he criticized western colonialism and took his point of departure from his sympathy with the movement to emancipate Asia and make it independent. On these points, Ōkawa's anti-colonialist Pan-Asianism makes sense. Because Japan was also part of the weak and the discriminated in the international community, a sense of solidarity with Asia was definitely possible.

However, Ōkawa's thought turned elsewhere. Japan was able to modernize and consolidate the state power necessary for resisting the west, ahead of other Asian countries. Thus, he began taking the stance that only through Japanese leadership could Asia be emancipated, and that Japan had the divine mission to fulfill that role.

Ōkawa argued that if Japan did not fulfill that role, Asia, being backward and weak, would quickly fall prey to the West. Thus, it is essential that Japan, the leader of Asia, strengthen its state power. Japan's advance into Asia is thus of a different character from the invasion of the western colonists. The former is driven by the need for Japan to unify Asia in order to be able to resist the west. In this way, he justified the Japanese invasion of Asia as the only path toward Asian emancipation.

During this time, Ōkawa was famous for calling this attitude of Japan, "Mahāyāna." It is "Hīnayāna" that pursues the spiritual freedom of the individual alone. But Mahāyāna takes a broad perspective and seeks out the liberation of the world. He said that what Asia needed to be is a "Mahāyāna Asia." But at the end of the day, what was this "Mahāyāna" really about? In actuality, was it not just the rationalization of Japanese aggression that merely brought suffering to the countries in Asia?

The term "Mahāyāna" was often used during the war in this way, as a pretext for Japan's invasion of other countries. Doing something not merely for one's own interests but for the sake of the other seems to be so magnanimous. But nobody wants that sort of interference. And that logic is not confined to the errors of the past. America's reasoning that the death of innocents is a necessary collateral damage required for ending Saddam Hussein's dictatorship and promoting democracy... That seems terribly familiar.

The demonic (*ma*) and resentment (*han*) are not individual problems alone. It is particularly when they rise to the level of national or state problems that troubling issues arise—problems which cannot be resolved rationally within the level of *ningen*. We have to be careful not to overlook the dirty reality behind superficial, romanticized discourses.

19

Rethinking the Relationship of Kami and Buddhas

On the religious dimension, the problem of Japanese nationalism directly connects with the problem of Shinto. However, one cannot simply dismiss Shinto as mere nationalism. It connects to a deeper sphere of the indigenous. Japanese religion developed for a long period as a syncretism of Shinto and Buddhism. Because of this, even from the standpoint of Buddhism, we cannot look at Shinto as some separate religion and pay no mind to it. Incidentally, in the Buddhist world, or amongst Buddhologists, Shinto and the kami[28] of Japan have not been discussed directly. Even if one goes through the writings or textbooks of great scholars in Buddhist Studies, one finds that the problems of the syncretism of Shinto and Buddhism (just like funeral Buddhism) are omitted.

After the war, D. T. Suzuki quickly embarked on a vehement critique of the war, and blamed the aggressions on Shinto. Furthermore, in progressive post-war scholarship, people praised the attitude of not worshiping kami in the Pure Land school, and considered the syncretism of Buddhism and Shinto as a defiling compromise that contaminated Buddhism. Of course, we have to consider the background of this. In the prewar period, State Shinto was the central ideology of statism and imperialism, and was a strong force for driving the people of Japan to war. Because of this, the prejudice took root that Shinto

28. ["Kami" can be translated as "God" or "gods." As the ambiguity is crucial for this word, I retain it in untranslated form.]

is dangerous thought. And unfortunately, for a long period, talking about Shinto was considered taboo. With the exception of a very small number of conscientious scholars like Yanagita Kunio and Origuchi Shinobu, there were no sufficiently productive discussions of Shinto.

However, the critique of this syncretism did not begin merely in the postwar period. Rather, at the start of the Meiji period, the government enforced the separation of Shinto and Buddhism, and the two religions emerged from their vague syncretism as separate entities. But this was Shinto rejecting Buddhism, which came from Shinto's attempt to realize the unity of rituals and state practice. That developed into an anti-Buddhist movement called "abolish Buddhism, destroy Śākyamuni."[29] Both the anti-Buddhist movement and the unity of religion and politics came to an end, but the separation of Shinto and Buddhism was maintained all the way up until the present, and has become entrenched.

SHIMAJI MOKURAI'S SEPARATION OF BUDDHISM AND SHINTOISM

This policy of separating Shinto and Buddhism was not particularly resisted by Buddhists. Rather, in some cases, it was even actively taken up. One example of this sort of reception came from Shimaji Mokurai, a great leader of the True Pure Land school in the early part of the Meiji period.

Shimaji directly criticized the religious integration policies of the Institute for Religious Education of the Meiji government. He argued that religion should not be controlled by the state, and the True Pure Land school became independent from the Institute for Religious Education. This is commonly known as the first incidence of the establishment of modern religious freedom in Japan. After this affair, religious freedom was enshrined within the Meiji Constitution, and gradually

29. 廃仏毀釈.

took hold. Shimaji took the stance of religious evolutionism and criticized polytheistic Shinto as a low level of religion. He saw Buddhism as a higher form of religion, and tried to demarcate the two. Thus, on this point, he supported the separation of Shinto and Buddhism.

I will leave the discussion of some serious issues in Shimaji's view for a later time. Perhaps Shinto is a primitive and lower kind of religion. But even if we ignore the religious aspect, it is quite meaningful as something that gives honor to the emperors and subjects who built Japan. And certainly, this way of thinking guided the later theory that Shinto is not a religion, which was promoted by the Meiji government. This implies that if Shinto is not a religion, then its enforcement does not conflict with religious freedom. This is none other than State Shinto.

THE MUTUALLY COMPLEMENTARY STRUCTURE OF SHINTO AND BUDDHISM

In this way, the separation of Shinto and Buddhism resulted in Buddhism's independence from Shinto and its recognition as a "pure religion." However, because Shinto was not considered to be a religion, there were no issues with it existing alongside Buddhism either. (In the present, while the syncretism of Shinto and Buddhism is no longer considered valid, there is still absolutely no problem with Japanese people aligning with both. As a matter of fact, that is considered to be the most natural thing to do.) Buddhism, a religion, was concerned with the individual. And Shinto, a non-religion, was concerned with the state. The two had a division of roles that was free from contradiction.

As we see, while taking a different form from the previous syncretism, Shinto and Buddhism coexisted once again in this bi-layered division of roles. In order to distinguish this from "Shinto- Buddhist syncretism" (*shinbutsu shūgō*), I refer to this as "Shinto-Buddhist complementation" (*shinbutsu hokan*). So long as they were on different dimensions, Buddhism could not spout criticisms against or meddle with Shinto. Rather, Buddhism began supporting State Shinto from the background.

This stratified, mutually complementary structure was not sufficiently reconsidered even after the war, and its problems have remained tucked away. From now on, it is necessary to dig up and investigate these issues. However, there is something we ought to be careful about here. In the post-war period, Shinto was no longer enforced by the government and became just one of many religions. But despite this, looking at it on the level of the faith of ordinary people, the new form of Shinto and Buddhist complementation continues.

Even today, many people visit both shrines and temples, feeling no sense of contradiction in that. Previously, a good number of "intellectuals" argued against this, saying that it shows a lack of constancy in religion, or that people lack true faith. This sadly resulted in the ordinary people, who have this layered faith in kami and buddhas, guiltily feeling that their own faith is inferior. But there are many forms to faith, and one cannot dictate which one is superior to the others.

Furthermore, the present relationship between Shinto and Buddhism is hardly anarchic. The mutual division of roles is quite clear: When one is born, one goes to the shrine. The festivals for children aged seven, five, and three, weddings—all auspicious events and initiation ceremonies tied to the development of a human being—are presided over mainly by Shinto. Ceremonies like funerals and memorial services—things related to mourning and death—are in the jurisdiction of Buddhism. This is the presiding division of labor, and in this way, Shinto and Buddhism have truly formed a system of healthy complementarity. This system of division of labor already began in the Heian period (794–1185) and one can say that it has deeply permeated the Japanese psyche. Today, weddings are more often held in Christian fashion. Thus, the structure of Shinto, Buddhism, and Christianity has become all the more complex.

Considering this mutually complementary structure of Shinto and Buddhism, it would be a mistake, arrogance, to think that Buddhism can completely fulfill the role of religion on its own. Buddhism and Shinto both have their strengths and weaknesses. As we can see from their system of division of labor, Buddhism's advantage is that it deals with death and the afterlife well, and it has become established as funeral Buddhism. In contrast, its weakness lies in the dynamic response toward the activities of life, which it tends to lack. The tendency toward denying the secular world is originally strong in Buddhism, and it is particularly rejecting of sex and reproduction, which it has been hard pressed to sufficiently give value to. While there are trends toward a more positive approach in Japanese *hongaku* thought and esoteric Buddhism, these trends tend to be seen as corruptions.

On the flip side, Shinto originally lacked funeral rites and has not sufficiently responded to the problem of the afterlife. Shinto funeral rites were made by imitating funeral Buddhism; despite that, Shinto funerals have yet to see widespread use. But conversely, Shinto has many elements that arise from indigenous agricultural ceremonies, and naturally, in these elements, we have the desire for bountiful harvest, reproductive fertility, and the prosperity of one's descendants. Because of this, Shinto emphasizes sex and reproduction, shows a love for life, and greatly values child-rearing and education.

Toward a dialogue with indigenous kami

As we see, Buddhism and Shinto have opposite value systems, and it is difficult to simply synthesize them. Because of this, there is no way for Japan to naively return to the Shinto-Buddhist syncretism of old. However, it is precisely because of this that we can make use of the strengths of each and make their mutual complementation even more productive. Recently, interreligious dialogue has become a buzzword, and there has been much dialogue between Buddhism and Christianity, or Shinto and Christianity. But quite sadly, Buddhism and Shinto, who have the deepest mutual relationship, have not been afforded sufficiently productive discussion with each other.

This might seem strange, but historically, Shinto and Buddhism have had a rather warped relationship, and perhaps they have difficulty trusting each other. Particularly after the Edo period, Shinto became more nationalistic and strengthened its anti-Buddhist stance, rejecting Buddhism as something alien to Japan. From there, it is a fact that Shinto often got mired in an intolerant nationalism and worship of the emperor, eventually leading to State Shinto. Even today, such a tendency is still present, and it would be ill-advised to accept it in its present form.

On the other hand, does Buddhism's world religious character make it superior to Shinto, which is a folk religion? I do not think so. History gives ample evidence that world religions are often turned into pawns for political domination. Buddhism may not seem as extreme as the case of Christianity, but since the ancient period, factually speaking, Buddhism was often used for the benefit of those in power. When it comes to the relationship of Shinto and Buddhism, their syncretism has, in most cases, taken place with Buddhism (which had the strength of foreign cultures behind it) subjugating indigenous kami and making them subordinate to Buddhism.

Of course, during that process, the indigenous kami also gained in influence, and so one cannot say that the kami were simply overpowered by the buddhas. However, it is important to note that the more Shinto developed into a large-scale religion, the somewhat parallel-dimensional character originally possessed by the indigenous kami, which appeared and disappeared within everyday life, tended to fade. In the beginning, indigenous kami could be glimpsed only within subtle transformations within nature. If one did not possess fine sensibilities and did not concentrate deeply, they could not be seen. The same is true for our deceased loved ones. (I will discuss this in Part III.)

If one ignores these little gods and the dead, and tramples them underfoot, then well, that is that. While it may seem as if State Shinto emphasized the kami, was it not actually a process of trampling on the gods for the sake of political ends? There is no need to say where that led. What trans-ethics aims at is none other than a reconsideration of the dead and the kami as other, where otherwise, they have merely been fodder for the politics and ethics of *ningen*.

20

Can We Restore Nature?

Nowadays, it is not just the domain of *ningen* that is in a state of crisis but nature as well. The environment is becoming more and more polluted, the earth is becoming dangerously warm, and there seems to be no stopping it. The excessive consumption of forms of energy, the production of carbon dioxide, the destruction of forests... Ecosystems are being destroyed, and the circle of life is going haywire. Destruction of the ozone layer, pollution from pesticides, medicines, chemicals, and particularly, endocrine disruptors and waste and exhaust gases—all these problems have gone beyond the limit, and the Earth is groaning. Atomic energy, which was touted as an all-powerful source, is not only dangerous in itself, but produces the most dangerous nuclear waste. We may seem to be dealing with it for now, but we are passing the buck to future generations.

In contrast, what has science accomplished? Until a certain point in the post-war period, the future of humankind seemed brimming with hope. Rising up from war, the Japanese thought that humankind would never repeat the idiocy of war, and that through a positive use of science, we could head toward a peaceful and abundant world. This sort of hope rang not just in Japan but all over the world. People thought that science would bring a rosy future. America and the USSR competed, and we had astronauts and cosmonauts, even men on the moon. It seemed like if the Earth got overpopulated, all we needed to do was fly into space and open up so much more new possibilities.

However, we quickly learned that reality is not so sweet. Although an enormous amount of funds was used for space development, we find that in the harsh conditions outside Earth, humanity would not fare well. Maybe humankind, or perhaps even life itself, cannot live except by clinging to this measly planet we call Earth. There seems to be no escaping these harsh realities.

If that is the case, then how have things fared with the progress of medicine, which concerns itself directly with our lives? Certainly we have many new medical treatments, like organ transplants, and many diseases previously deemed untreatable are now no longer so. Our ability to prolong life has increased in a big way. However, on the flip side, new diseases seem to keep popping up: AIDS, SARS, mad cow disease, avian flu... Medicine seems to chase after diseases as in an endless game of tag. It seemed like everything would be possible, from genetic engineering to perhaps even cloned human beings. But nobody can welcome these discoveries without trepidation. Ought human beings be fiddling with the very foundations of life?

The mysteries of nature seem like they ought to have been exhausted by now, but rather, today, nature threatens humankind even more fiercely, as if seeking vengeance. Perhaps we could call this the *han* (resentment) of nature. While science has had human prosperity as its marketing slogan, has it not done the opposite, and brought us the means of humankind's destruction? When one opens Pandora's box, there is no closing it. The reason we say that the contemporary era began with Auschwitz, Hiroshima, and Nagasaki is because with these, a huge turn for the future of humankind took place. What the Nazis tried to effect was a restructuring of the natural species called "humanity," and the atom bomb the US developed made the destruction of humankind possible. The various attempts to avoid such a crisis have yet to succeed. There is no more stopping the rampage of science.

THE DEATH OF THE PLANET

The famous physicist, Stephen Hawking, is known to have predicted that humankind would be destroyed within a thousand years. For sure, in the past, these "end times" narratives have been repeated over and over again. And it even seems like it is the optimistic views of human progress that were no more than a fluke phenomenon from the nineteenth to the twentieth century. However, the contemporary conditions are not simply a repetition of these theories of the eschaton. Rather, what we have are much more severe issues, which are clear to anyone who looks.

Of course, as all existence is impermanent, it would not make sense if humankind were the only exception. Just as the death of an individual is inevitable, because humankind arose from nature, it must eventually perish. Not only that—the earth and this universe itself have a set lifespan, and are not eternal. According to the worldview of the Abhidharma (Pali. Abhidhamma) there is a four-part cycle to the universe that is endlessly repeated: the destruction of the universe (the *kalpa* of destruction), the continuing of a state of emptiness (the *kalpa* of nothingness), birth of a universe (the *kalpa* of formation), and its continuity (the *kalpa* of existence). It is said that when the *kalpa* of existence ends, the three calamities of fire, water, and wind will come. This is a large-scale myth that reminds us of Nietzsche's idea of eternal recurrence. However, it is not just a myth; the death of the universe is seen as inevitable even by science.

Looking at it from the religious dimension, this eschaton does not come in the future, but rather must be thought of in the space of the present moment. In the twenty-ninth case of *The Blue Cliff Record*, we have the discussion of the koan "Daizui's 'It Will Be Gone with the Other." A *kalpa* fire is a great fire sweeping across the universe that comes at the end of the *kalpa* of existence (where the world is in a state of stable continuity). A monk asked Daizui, "When the kalpa fire flares up and the great cosmos is destroyed, I wonder, will 'it' [this fundamental thing] perish, or will it not perish?" Daizui answered, "It will perish." The monk then shows his strong side, saying, "Then I'll go with it." But Daizui rejects him bluntly, saying, "then go." If it were just an imagined end of the world in the future, then you can jump into it.

However, if right here, right now, you are really forsaken, could you bear it?

Of course, this is an eschaton on the religious level and not necessarily an actual problem. No point in worrying now about the end of the universe, which will happen very far into the future. However, the end of humankind and the earth are, at this point, well within the scope of our consideration. Thinking of the death of humankind is, far more than thinking of the death of an individual, terrifying to the point of absurdity. If the individual dies, then perhaps what one leaves behind can be taken up by one's children. But if humankind as a whole perishes, then in such a future, there is no comfort to seek.

THE RELATIONSHIP BETWEEN THE KAMI OF JAPAN AND NATURE

That being said, our main concern for the moment is, rather than being terrified about such an annihilation, finding out how to put the brakes on the destruction of nature and how to preserve the environment on Earth. These past few years, some scholars have idealized the animism of ancient Japan as an ecological philosophy. But I doubt if things are that simple. In the first place, it is not clear if we can call the religion of ancient Japan an "animism." Recently, I have come to think that perhaps the way of thinking that mountains, waters, grasses, and trees are all kami (or buddhas) may have begun with the introduction of Buddhism and the theory that grasses and trees attain Buddhahood (*sōmoku jōbutsu*).

Originally, people did not think that kami were natural phenomena themselves, but rather that they were the extraordinary existences lurking behind natural phenomena. Kanno Kakumyō writes, "The 'kami' of our country are the things from the other side (*uragawa*) that show themselves as the scenery."[1] This means, kami cannot be seen so

---

1. Kanno Kakumyō 菅野覚明『神道の逆襲』[The counterattack of Shinto] (Tokyo:

long as we look at nature from the point of view of the architectonic of *ningen*. In this sense, they are the same as the dead. Kami are at the boundary of the order of *ningen*, or they show themselves through fine cracks in the world of *ningen*. This is why kami are often depicted as showing themselves as snakes. In this way, they show themselves as foreign beings in the gaps of the order of *ningen*, suddenly glimpsed, only to disappear as quickly as they came—envoys of another world in "the other side."

However, to be certain, the kami are not divorced from nature. The mountains, trees, and rocks in nature are the *yorishiro* (representatives or dwelling places) of kami, and these mediate between people and kami. Because of this, nature is related to kami, and people regarded these natural objects with awe and treated them with care. Forests and swamps were also thought to be the dwelling places of kami. Pushing this further, we can say that nature itself is an other that deviates from the bounds of *ningen*, and is beyond the reach of human power.

Is *SŌMOKU JŌBUTSU* A PHILOSOPHY OF RESPECTING NATURE?

With the arrival of Buddhism to Japan, the theory that "Grasses, trees, the country—all these attain Buddhahood" developed from that of the theory of Buddha-nature. This notion that plants and land attain enlightenment is a development of the idea of Buddha-nature that is particular to Japan. These words first occur in Annen's (ca. 841–?) *Private Record of Examinations and Theories on Grasses and Trees Attaining Buddhahood*. There is something noteworthy in this work, even when seen from the history of thought. The theory of grasses and trees attaining Buddhahood was also put forth in China, but its basis was that if subjects with feelings (sentient beings) attained enlightenment, then the environment of grasses and

---

Kōdansha Gendai Shinsho, 2001).

trees—which do not feel—would attain Buddhahood as well. This idea is still somewhat aligned with the core principles of Buddhism, which have the enlightenment of sentient beings in mind. However, for Annen, it is these insentient grasses and trees themselves that each resolve to attain enlightenment, and then become buddhas. This is a really strange way of thinking. What might this mean?

Annen did not resolve this problem himself, but rather it was first resolved in the development of the doctrine of *hongaku* in the Tendai school. Here, it says that plants germinate, flower, bear fruit, and wilt. This very process is, as it is, the resolve to attain enlightenment, the spiritual practice, and the awakening of the plants. In this way, each process in nature is accorded respect as being, in itself, a manifestation of the Buddha. This view arose from the philosophy of mandalas (from Esoteric Buddhism) being taken in by Shugendō (Japanese mountain asceticism). Together with the view that hills and mountains are in themselves mandalas, these philosophies deeply influenced the Japanese view of nature. However, it would be foolish to immediately sing the praises of these philosophies as ecological (in the sense of giving respect and value to nature). On the flipside of the philosophy of "nature as it is" is the irresponsible attitude that belittles human effort and just accepts things as they are and becoming as they become.

Although Japan has been blessed by an abundance of nature, it has become a "developed nation" when it comes to the destruction of nature and polluting the environment, thanks to the hurried and haphazard economically reductionist development in the post-war period. Nature is also "other" to us, and we cannot feel its pain and listen to its lament from within the purview of the ethics of *ningen*. Deep ecologists argue that nature has the same rights as human beings. This way of thinking has a point, but it puts nature within the framework of *ningen*. I do not think it is enough to see nature as equal to humans. Nature is something we share with the dead and the kami, and is not something to be monopolized by the living. The question of how to deal with nature is another thing that needs to be considered from the point of view of trans-ethics.

Part Three

From the Other to the Dead

21

The Dead as the Extreme Limit of the Other

Even though we must inevitably encounter the other, this encounter is unpredictable and it deviates from the "betweenness of persons." We can think of the dead as the ultimate form of such an other. Between living persons, people can discuss, adjust their opinions, and decide upon rules. However, one cannot argue with the dead. Because of this, one cannot possibly reduce this encounter to the rules of *ningen*. However, we all live relating with the dead in some form or another. Such a troublesome other. The other cannot be comprehended through ethics; it inevitably becomes a trans-ethical problem. We have occasionally touched upon the problem of the dead; however, it must now be considered as the most central issue of trans-ethics.

Here, let me first touch upon the problem of death and the dead. Death has been a constant theme in philosophy and religion. The issue of whether death is the end of all things or if there is life after death has long been an insoluble problem. One might say that it is a pointless argument. If one asked Buddha, he would say it is *avyākṛta* (unanswerable); and Kant agrees that this issue cannot be solved by pure reason. In this way, death was expelled from the realm of philosophical problems.

However, perhaps the problem has simply been set up all wrong. Because the circumstance of death is set up as the utmost limit, no matter how far one goes, one cannot go beyond that point. This is the same as the philosophical argument concerning solipsism. If we think of the existence of the "I" as a singular starting point, then not only the other, but the rest of the external world, becomes uncertain. This world may just be my dream, or a hallucination. If this were the case, the only certain thing becomes my own consciousness. In Buddhism, the philosophy of *yuishiki* (consciousness only, S. *vijñapti-mātratā*) developed in this direction.

However, if we alter our perspective a little bit, this solipsism becomes very unreasonable. In reality, we communicate with others through words. Whether it be a dream or a hallucination, the fact that we are dealing with others is a reality. When we think of it this way, the very idea of questioning the absolute certainty of the other's existence becomes strange. Instead, we must take the fact that we are involved with others as our point of departure, and ask, how might we be able to relate with others better?

PEOPLE LIVE IN RELATION WITH THE DEAD

Considering the refutation of solipsism, perhaps the perspective from which we view the problem of death needs to be changed as well. As long as one comprehends death as a circumstance that limits the self, it is inevitable that one hit a deadlock and thus be unable to make intellectual progress beyond the idea of death. However, if we take the fact that we already live in relation with the dead as our starting point, then it is no longer a barren abstract discussion, but rather something that everyone experiences.

Perhaps some might argue that they have no relationship with the dead. It is often said that funerals are for the living, not for the dead. However, I think those who have experienced the death of someone close can understand that this is not a simple matter. The absence of the dead, in the very fact of their absentness, inevitably attains an infinite gravity. The dead speak to us with silent messages, and declare the factuality of their absence before us. The living have no choice but to relate with the absent and unspeaking dead. The relationship with the dead is certainly part of our experience. It is not just our interpretation of things, nor merely an illusion.

Of course, this is not to be taken simply as a theory that after death, existence continues as it did in life. For example, we have the view of life and death that sees Amitābha's Pure Land as a paradise that lies in the distant west, and that after death, one goes there. Or we have the view where one is invited by God to enjoy eternal happiness in heaven. It is not necessarily wrong to believe in these outright, if one can. However, even someone who believes such, when faced with the death of a loved one, is certainly overwhelmed by a feeling of infinite absence. This is by no means mere theory. Before starting off from some theoretical point of view, I think we must begin from the inescapable reality we sense and intuit.

A relationship with a dead person is, of course, different from a relationship with a living being. It is impossible to communicate with the dead as one would with a living being. A relationship with a dead person takes place in the very space where "inter-personal" communication becomes impossible. I say this not as a theory, nor from one particular faith, but rather as a matter of fact.

Also, the relationship with the dead changes over time. The dead are gradually forgotten and the relationship becomes tenuous. But also, there are times when the dead are not merely absent but lovingly watch over the living. However, it is not always the case that the dead merely give comfort to the living. Some dead forever persecute the living, as the dead in Auschwitz and Hiroshima do. There are the dead who forever indict the human race.

If living beings have a relationship with the dead, then conversely, the dead also have a relationship with living beings. Otherwise, the relationship of living beings to the dead would simply be a subjective impression or a hallucination. The dead neither sink into oblivion, nor do they live eternally, somewhere separate from living beings. And so, rather than thinking of "death" as running up against the edge of life and falling from it into nothingness, is it not more appropriate to think of death as a turning or transition from *being* one of "the living" to *being* one of "the dead?"

How to relate with the Buddha as one of the dead

Earlier, we tried to read the first half of *The Lotus Sutra* as a theory of the other (Chapter 15). Again, let us use *The Lotus Sutra* as an entry point to get closer to the problem of the dead. Interestingly, the theme of the second half of this text is none other than the dead as the other, so if we read from the first half to the second, its structure is that of a theory of the other progressing to a theory of the dead. The beginning of the second half is "Chapter x. The Expounder of the Dharma," but from there, the death (and subsequent entry into *nirvāṇa*) of Buddha is taken up as the main problem. Upon the death of Buddha, it is none other than *The Lotus Sutra* that becomes the substitute for Śākyamuni. It is recommended that one "remember, read, chant, explain, and transcribe each phrase."

If the theme of the first half is the encounter with (Śākyamuni) Buddha as the other, the theme of the second half is the problem of how we are able to relate with the same Buddha (who has now entered final *nirvāṇa*) as one of the dead. With the death of Buddha, we may say that his existence is one that is in the "past." Yet from a Buddhist perspective, we are not really separate from Buddha, for Buddha is imminent in his absence. In place of the Buddha, in his absence, we have *The Lotus Sutra*. In relating with this text, for the first time, a person can become the messenger of the Tathāgata, and a relationship with Buddha again becomes possible.

The central focus of the second half is the sequence from "Chapter xi. The Appearance of a Jeweled Stupa," to "Chapter xv. Bodhisattvas Emerging from the Earth" and up until "Chapter xvi. The Lifespan of the Tathāgata." Here, the relationship with the deceased Buddha is taken up more assertively. Even though it is commonly Chapter xvi that is mainly considered through this kind of point of view, I think that perhaps Chapter XI should be emphasized more. In this chapter, the deceased Prabhūtaratna Tathāgata appears. Prabhūtaratna Tathāgata is the Tathāgata who lived in the past, in a land "tens of millions of billions of countless worlds to the east" called "Treasure Purity," and had already passed away. However, his body was kept in a stupa, and he had vowed that wherever *The Lotus Sutra* is preached, he would appear. And so when Śākyamuni preached this sutra, Prabhūtaratna Tathāgata came from afar to attend.

Prabhūtaratna Tathāgata is one of the dead. In that chapter, Śākyamuni sits beside Prabhūtaratna Tathāgata in his stupa. This is called "Two Seated Buddhas," and is a frequently depicted scene in paintings and sculptures. It is when the living Śākyamuni comes together with the dead Prabhūtaratna Tathāgata that the former's authentic power is first manifest. This shows that living beings do not live merely among the living, but that they also need the power and the energy of the dead. The idea that the living live merely among the living is a form of arrogance. The dead perpetually censure and challenge us.

BODHISATTVAS AS ONE WITH THE DEAD

In "The Appearance of a Jeweled Stupa," Śākyamuni's acceptance of the dead Prabhūtaratna Tathāgata is in itself a call for bodhisattvas to accept Buddha, after his passing, as one of the dead. Here, the idea of the bodhisattva undergoes a major shift from the first half of *The Lotus Sutra*. In the first half, a bodhisattva is one who cannot possibly exist without the other. However, in the second half, that is no longer sufficient to be a bodhisattva. In order for a bodhisattva to be a bodhisattva, he or she must relate with the dead.

This must be surprising, and perhaps is difficult to accept. Rationally considered, we can admit that people cannot live without others. But why does one have to have a relationship with the dead? At this point, religion decisively goes beyond the realm of ethics "between persons." (Similarly, the importance of the image of the crucified Christ implies the central role of accepting the dead in Christianity.)

In the previous view of bodhisattvas, the idea of bodhisattvas existing along with the dead was unthinkable. There was a need for a new kind of bodhisattva; and this is the theme of "Chapter XV. Bodhisattvas Emerging from the Earth." The new notion of bodhisattvas that appears here is one of bodhisattvas who come out from the earth. They are bodhisattvas who have been guiding those in this world since before Śākyamuni attained enlightenment.

If it is just a matter of Śākyamuni's having preached even during his previous lives, then the same is true for Śāriputra and the other disciples (discussed in Part 1 of *The Lotus Sutra*), who would have been listening to his teachings as well. If so, I do not think there is any real change with the "bodhisattvas emerging from the earth," nor is there a need for new bodhisattvas to emerge. I think it is mistaken to see the bodhisattvas that emerged from the earth as being different from the bodhisattvas up until then. They are no different from Śāriputra and the others, and for us as well, who are also bodhisattvas. However, the character of the bodhisattva is different from the first half. There is a shift in the essence of being a bodhisattva. This was expressed as the emergence of new bodhisattvas.

In this manner, the chapter on "The Lifespan of the Tathāgata" presupposes "The Appearance of a Jeweled Stupa," and "Bodhisattvas Emerging from the Earth." In "The Lifespan of the Tathāgata," Śākyamuni clarifies, "I became a buddha long ago, immense and limitless ten million billion ages have passed." He says that he had attained Buddhahood in the immeasurably distant past. This is precisely what has been taken as the fundamental truth of the "main gate" (the latter half) of *The Lotus Sutra*. However, as I have said before, this cannot be established merely through "The Lifespan of the Tathāgata." First, it needs to be based upon the establishment of cooperation with the dead, as we see in "The Appearance of a Jeweled Stupa." Then, it requires the shift in the essential concept of a bodhisattva found in

"Bodhisattvas Emerging from the Earth." Only then can we have the powerful other, the dead, understood as the previously enlightened (*kuon jitsujō*) Śākyamuni, as seen in "The Lifespan of the Tathāgata."

Therefore, this figure of Śākyamuni is both Buddha, an absolute being, and the extreme form of the other = the dead. Seen from the latter point, he is not a special being. The dead are others, more deserving of awe than the living, overwhelming us, drawing us into a relationship with them. While we may be frightened by the dead, if we accept them and come to terms with our existence alongside them, a previously unseen new world will open up.

22

Relating to the Dead

Tanabe Hajime (1885–1962) is known as a philosopher of the Kyoto School who developed his own unique philosophy while criticizing his senior, Nishida Kitarō. He began his career doing neo-Kantian philosophy of science. But through his criticism of Nishida, he deepened his philosophy concerning issues regarding the state and ethics, which were weak points of Nishida. However, his career met a severe setback due to his wartime cooperation, and he turned his focus to religion. He started afresh and renewed his previous philosophical system in his book *Philosophy as Metanoetics* (1946), which was charged with his faith in Shinran. Coupled with the then current tide of repentance concerning the war, this book exerted considerable influence.

Tanabe spent his later years deepening his religious philosophy, even after this work. He was sympathetic to Christianity and also looked into Zen. However, unlike Nishida's philosophy, which was based on an experience of Zen, Tanabe's philosophy did not have a strong religious foundation. He also shuttled back and forth between Buddhism and Christianity. Because of these, his religious philosophy was not received very well. This is particularly true of his "philosophy of the dead," which he developed in his final years. This work is epoch-making—the first to establish the interaction with the dead philosophically. However, for a long time, it was not given a fair assessment, largely because it was too far ahead of its time, and up until that time, the problem of the dead had been consistently ignored.

In 1951, upon his wife Chiyo's death, Tanabe wrote, "For my humble self, my wife has resurrected and forever lives within me."[2] From this experience, he developed a philosophy of existential communion with the dead, through their resurrection. Another event that made Tanabe ponder more deeply on the problem of death was the 1954 S. S. Lucky Dragon 5 nuclear exposure incident from the United States' nuclear testing on Bikini Atoll. Tanabe writes, "This so-called nuclear age is undoubtedly, literally the 'age of death'. It is not just that 'our days are numbered', but to put it strongly, one cannot even expect to survive another day."[3] Here we see his grave historical consciousness.

Tanabe's philosophical task lay in criticizing Heidegger. In the latter's definitive work, *Being and Time (Sein und Zeit)*, he argued that people can regain their authenticity only through anticipatory resoluteness toward death. This has been a very influential idea, but it only considers one's own death. However, as I have already mentioned, one's own death cannot be experienced. The only condition that can be experienced is "living-toward-death." No matter how much "anticipatory resoluteness" one has, as long as one is alive, one does not arrive at death. Death remains a yonder shore, cut off from life.

Does this mean that, at the end of the day, the religious problem of death and resurrection is nothing but nonsense? However, even if the dead cease to exist, the relationship with the dead does not disappear. Is this not precisely what is referred to as "death and resurrection?" If so, we require a philosophical theory that can explain this. This is precisely what Tanabe's "Philosophy of Death" provides.

Tanabe says, "What the dead had fervently wished for in life is, for the living, a love forever renewed even after the death [of the other]. This love works ceaselessly, mediated by the love of the living for the

2. Tanabe Hajime 田辺 元、一九五六年二月十二日野上弥生子宛書簡 [February 12, 1956, letter to Nogami Yaeko].

3. Tanabe Hajime,「メメント・モリ」[Memento mori].

dead. And as the mutual existential communion of love, it makes death and resurrection possible."[4]

The love of the dead continues to call upon the living despite their passing. This must be heeded, taken up by the living. As an example, Tanabe takes up Case 55 of *The Blue Cliff Record* ("Dōgo's 'I Would Not Tell You'"). This case tells the story of how the disciple Zengen, who at first did not understand his master Dōgo's teaching regarding life and death, was guided by Dōgo's teaching even after Dōgo's death, and finally attained enlightenment. Even in death, Dōgo's compassion continued to show his disciple the way.

In some parts, Tanabe's concept of existential communion with the dead tends to be romanticized. In reality, the interaction with the dead does not always go so smoothly. But despite these deficiencies, his straightforward discussion and "philosophizing" of our interchange with the dead (which had previously been ignored) is groundbreaking, making him a pioneer of the period.

WHY DO WE PRAY AT THE HOUSEHOLD ALTAR?

However, even without being brought up as a philosophical issue, interaction with the dead lives on within Japanese Buddhism as it is actually carried out. For example, many Japanese people place the mortuary tablets of deceased family members on their Buddhist household altars (*butsudan*), and perhaps see it as a place where the dead are enshrined. When I was young, this was how I (quite innocently) thought as well. However, I heard from a monk that the Buddhist household altar should exclusively enshrine Buddha as a principal image of worship—it is a mistake to make it a place of ancestor worship. I was just starting to learn Buddhist Studies during that time, and I thought that made sense.

---

4. Tanabe Hajime, 「生の存在論か死の弁証法か」 [An ontology of life or a dialectics of death?].

However, recently, I have been thinking, is this really the right way to look at it? I am no longer so certain. I currently live with my wife in a small apartment, and so we do not have a Buddhist household altar, although we do have a small Buddha installed. However, when I go back to my ancestral home and put my hands together in front of the household altar, I do not feel like I am putting my hands together for the enshrined Buddha. My parents are alive and well, so the mortuary tablets there are of my grandfather and grandmother. Since my grandfather died when I was young, I do not remember much of him. But I was a "grandma's boy," so when I go back to my ancestral home and put my hands together at the family altar, I think of my grandmother. A strong wave of nostalgia passes through me—as if I were greeting my grandma whom I miss dearly. As for my wife, her father passed away, and so when she puts her hands together in front of the household altar, not surprisingly, the feeling she has is one of greeting her father.

People may say that this is strange, but this is probably quite common among the Japanese. Even if we are told that this is wrong, and this practice ought to be abandoned, one cannot help but have these kinds of feelings, and it is hard to consider this as wrong. What wrong is there in taking care of the dead? Is it not more of a sacrilege toward the dead to treat their mortuary tablets as mere extras on the family altar?

How do we think about the soul after death?

I was very intrigued by a most interesting true story, found in the book of Sasaki Kōkan, a religious anthropology scholar.[5] He was invited as a lecturer in a temple support workshop sponsored by the Sōtō Religious Affairs Office in a prefecture in Japan, and the discussion turned to the problem of the soul. The chief of religious affairs

5. Sasaki Kōkan 佐々木宏幹『仏と霊の人類学』 [An anthropology of buddhas and spirits] (Tokyo: Shunjūsha, 1993).

said that originally, in Buddhism, people were not concerned about whether or not we have souls. But considering the case of Japan, where the rituals for the dead have a long history, he was of the opinion that the persistence of the soul after death cannot categorically be denied. However, the assistant chief objected to this. To admit that an eternal soul exists is a form of substantialism, and he argued that it is heresy. Then, upon being asked by the moderator his opinion on the matter, Sasaki said, "Both are true." Upon which, laughter and applause erupted from the assembly, and the matter was settled.

People have always problematized this ambivalence in Japanese Buddhism. Speaking from the point of view of the Buddhist principle of no-self, the assistant chief's assertion was probably correct. However, in reality, funeral Buddhism is practiced in Japan, and this cannot be denied. Recent studies show that not only in Japan, but in places such as India and even in China, Buddhism has taken part in rituals for the dead since early on. If that is the case, what the chief said was more realistic.

However, even if this is the case, is it really acceptable to end the argument by saying, "Both are true?" Performing rituals without a clear foundation for one's own ends, reasoning merely that it is Japanese tradition, and then taking a large amount of money as "offerings"—that is *swindling*. These are acts of none other than a dubious religion. And, more than anything, this is yet another sacrilege toward the dead. The dead are not to be treated so lightly.

FUNERAL BUDDHISM HAS A SPECIAL POSITION IN THE RELATIONSHIP WITH THE DEAD

Earlier, I agreed with the practice of funeral Buddhism, and argued that we should take it as our point of departure. However, that does not mean that we should accept funeral Buddhism in its present form and carry on as custom dictates. If religion merely rides the status quo and treats the dead as its prey, then it does not deserve to survive.

The importance of funerals lies in the fact that it is precisely through funerals that we relate most deeply with the dead, opening up a shared space with them. We cannot allow ourselves to be driven merely by the interests and circumstances of the living.

As I mentioned earlier, the root of religion is in the relationship with the other, and that the other with the strongest sense of alterity is the dead. In building a base here, one is able to penetrate beyond the fixed ethics of the "betweenness of persons" and really acquire the power to live. This was clarified in our close analysis of *The Lotus Sutra*. If so, one can say that, at least in the origin of Mahāyāna Buddhism, there was an idea that we start off from our relationship with the dead. Or, to say it more conservatively, that idea was at least conceivable.

Let us return once again to the problem of the dead. The important thing here is not the question on an intellectual level of what the objective state of a soul is, after death. When we look at our everyday lives as inter-personal matters, they seem guarded by a fixed framework. But in reality, things are not as stable as they may seem, and things constantly deviate from that framework. In this deviation, we relate with others, we relate with the dead. The relationship with the dead is an inescapable fact, not a problem to be proven objectively. Can we use this relationship as a starting point? While I am still in the midst of trial and error, this is the direction I am pursuing.

Because of this, I am not implying an acceptance of funeral Buddhism as "skillful means." Rather, this is an invitation to think upon the problem of religion using funeral Buddhism as the *sole* point of departure. Or at least, I hope to suggest that this sort of approach is also possible. Thus, Japanese Buddhism can draw closest to the root of the problem of religion because, as funeral Buddhism, it bears the possibility of possessing the strongest relationship with the dead. Japanese Buddhism occupies a very favorable position because of its relationship with the dead.

Of course, there are probably people who do not feel much of a sense of kinship with the dead. Perhaps this is even the case for most people. Some might say that it is unhealthy to keep thinking about problems like these. However, even if that were the case, we could not say that people can live in total indifference to the dead either. And so I think that, rather than avoid it, we have no other choice but to face it head on.

23

The Dead Support the Living

Although the problem of one's own death is important, this death is something that nobody has experienced for him or herself. One can do no more than conjecture about it. Ordinarily, the ones who give information to those unexperienced in something are those who have already experienced such a thing. But when it comes to death, well, one would be dead. Prior to the problem of *one's death*, we need to examine the problem of *the dead* up close.

When we say "the problem of the dead," we automatically think "memorial services" for the dead. Nowadays, practical questions surrounding funeral services, tombs, and memorials for victims of war and large scale disasters have become important issues. Of course, these are weighty matters. However, if these were all that mattered, it would be as if living beings could comprehend how to deal with the dead, and could think about them entirely within the scope of inter-personal rules. Naturally, deciding one's attitude towards things such as burials and one's own grave is not necessarily founded upon establishing the fundamental question of the relationship with dying and the dead.

However, at the base of the rules of the "betweenness of persons," there are things that cannot be clarified therein. The interaction with the dead is a matter that arises from that base. The narratives of the dead transgress the public dimension and go beyond the inter-personal. The question of the dead is not one that can possibly be answered via rational principles. Nevertheless, these things possess the power to shake the very foundations of inter-personal relations.

THE EXISTING DEAD SUPPORT
THE ORDER OF THIS WORLD

In the previous chapter, we took up Tanabe Hajime, who asserted that we should shift our problem from death to that of the dead. That point is really worth considering. Now, from the standpoint of psychiatry, I would like to take up Watanabe Tetsuo's *Death and Madness*.[6] Even though Watanabe is a scholar in the field of psychopathology, this book is not just a narrowly-focused book in that field. As the author writes:

> The problem of death has been entrusted to philosophy. The problem of the dead has been entrusted to religion. And the problem of insanity has been entrusted to medical science.... However, I would like to return to the academic standpoint prior to philosophy, religion, and medical science, and consider the difficult problems of death in madness, and the dead from the point of view of madness.[7]

These days, the academe is overspecialized. People can only converse and discuss if they stay within the range of words that are approved for use in their own "inter-personal" realm. Even religion has lost that intense destructive power it once had, and is now domesticated by the betweenness of persons. Its transgressions (like the Aum incident) flare up only to be hosed down and extinguished. However, can we truly pursue fundamental questions, cut up and divided in meek and obedient versions of religion, philosophy, and science? Are we not called to return to the standpoint prior to the specialization and organization of these three fields?

Watanabe takes up the problem of the dead as a starting point in order to seek out such an originary standpoint. His reason for this is, "One cannot experience death. But the living can experience

6. Watanabe Tetsuo 渡辺哲夫『死と狂気』[Death and madness] (Tokyo: Chikuma Gakugei Bunko, 2002); first published in 1991.

7. Ibid., 11.

the dead."[8] He had been treating patients of the grave mental disease, schizophrenia, for many years, and was involved in the treatment of a quite tragic patient who had accidentally killed his parents and children. In going through that, he noticed that those afflicted by such mental ailments are unable to appropriately recognize that the dead have a way of being *as dead* (which is distinct from their existence as living). The dead are the ones who support and underlie our world, and if one becomes unable to recognize this, one falls into madness. The dead play this very crucial role.

Watanabe continues, "The dead continue to historically structure the world of the living. It is the dead who assist and support the living in order to make living beings into a historical existence."[9] Concretely, what does this mean? "All the things that are necessary for human life in this world have been given by the dead. Religion, law, customs, ethics, the significance of life, the meaning of things, feelings, and most importantly, words—we are borne upon the backs of nameless, countless dead people."[10]

Certainly, our predecessors have constructed our world. However, if it were merely about that, would it not simply mean that our lives stand on the basis of what the dead accomplished when they were living (in the past)? Is it enough for us to respect what our predecessors accomplished and remember that? Is that not different from saying that the dead still exist, and that they still function amongst us?

However, Watanabe would respond to the contrary. "The dead as a memory and the dead as existing are two different ways of thinking, which cannot coexist in the same dimension. It is the existence of the dead, the existing dead, that is absolute and prior."[11] This is a very important point.

8. Ibid., 9.
9. Ibid., 33.
10. Ibid.
11. Ibid., 79.

The hubris of forgetting the power of the dead

From this point, allow me to foray beyond Watanabe's work. Let us consider the example of murder. If we think rationally and exclusively of the world of the living, the dead are already "past" existences, and therefore no longer exist in the present. All that remains are memories of them. If so, what happens to responsibility when someone is killed? Would there be any point to bearing responsibility, in the present, toward a past existent that remains merely in memories?

To the contrary, perhaps some will say that one has responsibility for murder because one inflicts grief and damage to the bereaved. However, if so, does that mean that it is alright to kill those who have no one to grieve for them? If so, one would end up approving of the murder of the homeless that often occurs these days.

Futhermore, another way of thinking argues that murder disrupts the order of society, and thus people have to be held accountable for it. If we allowed for murder without restriction, society would fall into chaos, and each person's life would be endangered. Because of this, murder is rejected and strictly punished. Within the ambit of "the betweenness of persons," this logic is most convincing. In this case, conversely, murder that protects the order of society—state-instituted capital punishment, in some cases, killing in war—is approved of. It is from this logic that some argue that, for the sake of the war against terror, even civilian lives can be sacrificed.

In actuality, the United States military is indiscriminately killing civilians in Iraq. Japan has also made decisions that allowed its citizens to be killed. Behind this is the way of thinking wherein no matter how much one kills, the dead merely become past existents, and so if through that, a "great cause" can be upheld and one can save face, then it is acceptable. If we think about things merely within the scope of the living, that may be a valid way of thinking. Of course, these would not be judged as crimes.

A more religious, metaphysical approach is also possible. In the idea of sanctity of life, the violation of this sanctity through murder is not permitted. However, if we follow this train of thought, a person who has been killed is a *past* existent. Therefore, the one who is already dead no longer has sanctity of life, and thus we end up in a situation wherein there is no need, in the present, to judge the crimes of the past.

The conception that sees the dead as existents of the past, which exist in the present merely as the memories of the living, seems to be a very rational, appropriate way of thinking. But considering the above, we see that things are not that simple. The dead relate with the world of the living *in the present*, and continuously preserve its order. The deceased watch lovingly over the living, or relentlessly blame us. When the living forget the power of the dead and start to think that the living live merely by their own power, we have the beginnings of the hubris of the living.

Putting this as a theory of time, the point is that the past is not merely something that has already "passed." Time is by no means a linear flow from the past to the present and to the future. The view that time can be grasped linearly is merely the perspective of "inter-personal" rules. The past that has passed does not pass—it stands still, it lingers. It bleeds into the present and resurrects in it. It supports the present, or it eats at it.

According to Watanabe, in madness, the dead cannot really be dead. His patient Ichirō (not the client's real name) may have killed his father. But it is not that he does not remember that. "Ichirō elaborately remembers how his father was on the verge of death or right after dying."[12] Rather than not remembering, Ichirō remembers it too clearly. However, "But in the end, it is a recollection of the body of his father on the verge of death, or a perception of the corpse. But as

12. Ibid., 80.

a deceased person, his father never comes up."[13] In other words, the father "did not transition from the living to the dead."[14]

LENDING AN EAR TO THE WORDS
THE DEAD CANNOT SAY

Watanabe develops his theory further, but due to space constraints, I cannot go too deeply into his ideas. In any case, one can see from our previous considerations that the dead support the "inter-personal" order of the living. However, the dead do not merely support this order, but also have the power to destroy it.

Once upon a time, people lived in awe of the dead, and went to great lengths to appease them. The living and the dead existed in a tensional relationship, within which they could not simply get along easily. Of all those who are other, the dead are the ones characterized by the most poignant alterity. However, with the rise of rationalism, people started to forget about the dead at a certain point, and began to make light of their power. They began to assert that the power of the dead was no more than a superstition, an illusion, and fell into the conceit of thinking that the living could build an inter-personal order by their power alone. But today, this conceit is under fierce criticism.

The dead do not, by any means, speak with the ordinary words of the "betweenness of persons." They can only speak through silence. It is the duty of the living to listen well to these unspeakable, silent words. However, how can we be certain that what the living "hear" from the dead are not merely convenient projections by the former? Are the living not just preaching their own selfish desires in guise of the words of the dead?

This doubt will never be cleared. There is no objective standard by which to judge for or against such questions. Perhaps one merely pre-

13. Ibid.
14. Ibid.

sumes to hear. But it is by constantly bearing this anxiety that we are able to give heed, impartially, to the words of the dead.

24

The Restlessness of the War Dead

When the war in Iraq began, the "justice" of the United States' power marched boldly through opposition, and Japan happily followed suit, dispatching its Self-Defense Forces. Although intellectuals (the ones often called "romantics") opposed this, they did not have the power to sway public opinion.

Even in war, there are rules based on international law. Although many critics argued that the American invasion of Iraq had not abided by these rules, rules can be changed. Absolutely immutable rules would be problematic. And it is the strong, the victors, who create rules. This is the domain of the "inter-personal," after all. But it is a preposterous illusion to think that the United States, "the land of democracy," could never break rules. We must not forget that it was a constitution known as the most democratic in the world—the Weimar Constitution—that gave birth to Nazism.

Today, nobody believes that people simply learn from their past mistakes, act rationally, grow wiser, progress toward ideal society, and so forth. The Jewish philosopher Theodor Adorno showed us that the madness of Nazism was by no means a matter of chance, but rather was an inevitable fruit of modern rational enlightenment thinking. Adorno made quite an impact with his declaration, "To write poetry after Auschwitz is barbaric." He further posed a more fundamental question: "Can one live after Auschwitz?"[15]

15. See Theodor Adorno, *Negative Dialectics*, trans. by E. B. Ashton (London: Routledge and Kegan Paul, 1973).

We cannot think of contemporary problems without considering the dead of Auschwitz. However, if I may speak from my experiences of discussing with various people, the minute one brings up the problem of Auschwitz, silence descends. Then people duck the issue by saying, "You don't have to bring up something *that* extreme...." It is not that I have been to Auschwitz, and I do not have any specialized knowledge about it either. But if we take up Adorno's problematic, Auschwitz is by no means a problem exclusive to Nazis and Jews. It is a problem that casts its shadow over the entire contemporary period.

If there is something that sets apart Auschwitz from the brutality of other wars, it is that it was founded on eugenic philosophy, and was carried out in a totally systematic way, making full use of scientific means in order to try to annihilate an entire race. Compared to the "incidental" mass killing that occurs in the confusion of war, this was of a completely different nature. Auschwitz used to be unthinkable.

It is the atomic bombing of Hiroshima and Nagasaki that best corresponds to Auschwitz. On one hand, Auschwitz aimed at the eugenic excision of a race. On the other hand, the atomic bombs, while they were also meant to end the war, were an indiscriminate human experiment to test the ultimate weapon—nuclear weapons—developed by science. In that sense, more than Auschwitz, the atom bombs were the "glorious" product of modern rational science. They were its inevitable result.

People tend to think that Auschwitz, Hiroshima, and Nagasaki are problems of the past and not of the present. But that is mistaken. These events began the contemporary age. For example, the scientific philosophy of eugenics still continues with genetic manipulation, which is presently one of the fields at the cutting edge of science. The abortion of disabled fetuses found via prenatal testing has become difficult to control. I am not saying that these are identical to what the Nazis did, but there is a point to saying that, taken to its unrestricted extreme, it is quite close to what the Nazis had set out to do.

Furthermore, people may think that the problem of nuclear weapons has abated. But it still proliferates in a weakened form as depleted uranium bullets and the like. Chemical weapons are still being developed intensively. And as for the nuclear waste from nuclear energy, this problem remains unsolved, and we are hoping the later generations can foot the bill.

Science, which, as the apex of reason, ought to have brought happiness to humankind, has instead brought the greatest of tragedies. Auschwitz, Hiroshima, and Nagasaki were the starting points. The Aum Shinrikyō incident was no more than a miniature parody of these. There was a time when people bandied about the phrase "the end of history." But there is no mistaking it, the true end of history happened with Auschwitz, Hiroshima, and Nagasaki.

THE ETHICS OF MEMORY

Auschwitz, Hiroshima, and Nagasaki also made waves in the world of religion. The death of millions, crushed like insects, caused many to lose their faith in existing religions. In November 2003, Watanabe Tetsuo and the University of Tokyo's School of Literature (where I was based) held an integrated symposium on the theme, "The Cooperation Between the Dead and the Living," and we invited James Foard from Arizona University to give a talk.

Foard had spent many years studying the relationship between Hiroshima and Buddhism. In his lecture, he compared the cases of Auschwitz and Hiroshima, and argued that in both cases, existing religions could not explain the tragedy within their respective frameworks.[16] The Jews had accepted their previous hardship as tests by God. But that presupposes the survival of their nation. In the case of Auschwitz, if the nation

16. The topics of the talks of Foard and Watanabe can be found in 『死生学研究』 [Studies on death and life] (Autumn 2004).

itself perished, this explanation would have been rendered completely meaningless. Similarly, in Hiroshima, there were so many killed that one could not tell the remains of one person from the other. In such a case, the previous way of holding memorial services for the dead in Japan could not apply.

In these circumstances, Foard attempted to construct a new ethics, guided by the work of Avishai Marglit, an Israeli ethicist, whose book was entitled *The Ethics of Memory*.[17] Marglit's parents had sought refuge in Palestine, but the rest of his relatives in Europe perished in the hands of the Nazis. In the midst of this, without relying on religion, he pursued the question of how ethics might be possible after Auschwitz. I first came across Marglit's book thanks to Foard. I think that in light of contemporary ethics, it takes up grave and important problems.

In place of religion, Marglit argues for the importance of "memory." Memory is not just individual, there are also memories of a community. When considering this issue, Marglit distinguishes between "ethics" and "morality." "Ethics" occurs within "thick relationships," whereas "morality" occurs within "thin relationships." Thick relationships include one's parents, friends, lovers, people from the same hometown—relationships where feelings can be held in common. Thin relationships are more abstract, and the widest limit of this is the community of humankind, on the basis of a shared "humanity." Memories are shared in *thick* relationships and are passed on there. Such a community does not necessarily become a closed space. Rather, the key issue here is how to expand and continue the domain of ethics.

Marglit restricts his discussion to the general possibility of ethics. But at the base of this is the question of how the memory of the holocaust, as a memory of the community of the Jewish people, continues to found that ethics. This is a very concrete problem. But it is our memories of suffering, more than our pleasant memories, which

17. Avishai Marglit, *The Ethics of Memory* (Cambridge, MA: Harvard University Press, 2002).

are deeply etched into us. If we uphold these memories, can we still forgive? What happens if all those who remember die? There arise a host of difficult problems like these.

CAN WE HAVE ETHICS MERELY BY UPHOLDING THE MEMORIES OF THE LIVING?

I shall not go any further into Marglit's book. But reading it, I am impressed by the strength of his will to live through the memory of the holocaust and carry it forward to the future, without relying at all on religion. I am also moved by his severe sense of ethics. It is only by taking up the memories of the living and inheriting these memories that ethics becomes possible. It would be immensely difficult for us Japanese to meet such a severe demand.

I would be foolish to naively criticize this view. But one can, in the spirit of frankness, raise the question as to whether or not we can really bear the mantle of the dead merely by carrying on the memories of the living. Can we really be so certain of the power of the living? Can we accept consigning the dead to the oblivion of the past? Even considering the memories of the living, can these memories be maintained by the power of the living alone? I think that if those who have suffered and died do not lend their power to the living, there is very little the living can do on their own.

At the center of the Hiroshima Peace Park is a memorial stone for those who died in the atomic bombing. Upon it, the following well-known phrase is carved: "Rest in peace, for the mistakes shall not be repeated." The declaration of the living to the dead that we shall not repeat these mistakes is a very grave thing. Standing before this memorial stone, one falls silent. However, in the present, is it really alright for us to have the dead rest in peace? We have repeated these mistakes over and over again, and what is more, it is clear that these mistakes are getting worse and worse. Perhaps it was too optimistic to even think it possible to have the dead rest in peace while the living avoid repeating their mistakes.

The living are weak. Left to our own devices, we would repeat the most stupid, cruelest things, over and over again. And this pattern merely worsens. There is nobody to stop this save those who have suffered and died. The weathering and fading away of the significance of Hiroshima has long been spoken of. So long as we rely merely on the memories of the living, we cannot help but have them weather with time. If we cannot listen to the dead, if we cannot walk with the dead, then there is no stopping the devastation of the living.

25

The Limits of an Ethics without the Dead

In the previous chapter, I took up Avishai Marglit, who tried to construct an ethics without relying on religion, and ended up with the problem of memory. Allow me to take up another thinker who tried another way of constructing ethics without relying on religion: Karatani Kōjin, in his *Ethics 21*.[18] While Karatani also tried to suggest an ethics sans religion, he ended up with almost the exact opposite of Marglit's stance.

Karatani, like Marglit, also distinguishes between the ethics of "thick relations" and the morality of "thin relations," but using slightly different terminology. He writes, "I shall use the word morality (*dōtoku*) to refer to the norms of a community, and ethics (*rinri*) to refer to that which involves the duty of *freedom*."[19] In Karatani's parlance, it is thick relations that are for morality, and ethics is applied to thin relations. This makes for some confusing terminology, so I shall not be differentiating between "ethics" and "morality." In any case, while Marglit emphasizes thick relations, Karatani attempts to take the standpoint of Kantian ethics, which pursues the freedom of the human being unshackled by community.

In this way of thinking, humans are free. No matter how much deterministic inevitability there might be, one commits an act because one is free. And it is because of this that our responsibility becomes

18. Karatani Kōjin 柄谷行人『倫理21』[Ethics 21] (Tokyo: Heibonsha Raiburarī, 2003).

19. Ibid., 15.

an issue. Perhaps someone committed a crime because society is itself warped. But despite that, it is a person's free choice whether or not to go into crime. And thus we can challenge the responsibility of the person. This point of view definitely makes sense, and is completely correct so long as the rules of the "betweenness of persons" apply. However, when it comes to the problems I brought up, can these really be resolved merely by those rules? No matter how wonderful rules might be, it cannot be helped if they cannot be realized.

Karatani presupposes that ethics is established on a Kantian cosmopolitan standpoint. In Karatani's ethical stance, a person bears responsibility as an individual transcending the state and the nation. He considers the state as existing only as a subject of responsibility, and not as something that should be moved by interests or emotions. That is a commendable stance. Maybe virtuous people like Karatani can go anywhere in the world, and without prejudice, respond equally with reason and responsibility. However, how many people like these are there, really?

Are most people not first steered by feelings and interests? Furthermore, even if one is told that one ought to respond equally to all people, do our thoughts not first turn to those who we have "thick relations" with? No matter how many people are killed in Iraq—although for certain this may be a painful thought—it is the trivialities of office and home life that we perceive to be much more urgent and serious. To put it bluntly, it is normal to scowl at the terrible spectacle of Iraq on television, only to quickly forget it and think, "I wonder what's for dinner?" I do not think we can say this is mistaken.

Of course, there are people who are moved by the horrors of what is happening in Iraq, and unhindered by the moral risk, go for volunteer activities in the area. That is a wonderful thing. But that is something that is not necessarily decided via reason. Rather, perhaps it is more like succumbing to an unbearable urge of something that goes beyond reason. That would be entering into a "thick relationship" with the Iraqis. It is erroneous to think that people can ignore the emotions that create thick relations and act merely from reason.

THE DANGERS OF "METAPHYSICAL GUILT"

One of the books I am drawn to when I talk about the problem of war is Karl Jaspers' *The Question of German Guilt*. This book takes up the question of how the German people should take responsibility after World War II. He distinguishes four types of guilt: criminal guilt, political guilt, moral guilt, and metaphysical guilt. We could also call this guilt "responsibility." Here, the first three can be understood as belonging within the scope of *ningen*. But it is the fourth, metaphysical guilt, which I cannot seem to comprehend.

Of this he says that if one does not do everything in his power to prevent an offense, half of the guilt belongs to him or her.[20] This is a guilt (responsibility) that is related to "every injustice, every wrong in the world," and is thus similar to Kiyozawa Manshi's idea of responsibility for all things as one.[21] Just like the problems that beset Kiyozawa, the problem with this is that it is impossible for a finite individual. In Kiyozawa's case, one makes an about face and relies upon Amitābha instead, resulting in *irresponsibility*. Because of this, it is extremely dangerous to naively apply such a "responsibility toward everything." We need to be careful about how Japanese thinkers have uncritically bandied about Jaspers' "metaphysical guilt."

Instead, what goes beyond the domain of *ningen*, whether we want it to or not, are emotions, which cannot be regulated by reason. That is not a fourth kind of guilt (responsibility) to be added on top of the first three, but is rather of a completely different character. The first three can be judged using reason, and their rightness or wrongness can

20. Karl Jaspers, 『戦争の罪を問う』 [The Question of German Guilt], trans. by Hashimoto Fumio 橋本文夫 (Tokyo: Heibonsha, 1998), 49. See Karl Jaspers, *The Question of German Guilt*, trans. by E. B. Ashton (New York: Fordham University Press, 2000).
21. 万物一体の責任論.

be debated in the public sphere. In contrast, the fourth is an absurd, irrational thing, which cannot be brought up in public discourse. This is no longer ethics, but none other than the trans-ethical.

Previously, I referred to the episode about King Xuan of the kingdom of Qi, which is found in *Mencius*. Seeing a sacrificial ox being tugged along, King Xuan felt troubled for some reason. And he saved the ox and sacrificed a sheep instead. Thought about rationally, killing an ox and killing a sheep ought to be the same thing. But despite that, if he sees a cowering ox, he gets the urge to save it. (But no luck for the sheep, which he did not see.) Through the act of "seeing," the ox, who ought to have been none of his business, became something he bore a rather "thick" relationship with.

If somebody else's child were kidnapped, one would definitely feel pity for this person. But compared to the feeling of when one's own child is kidnapped, the gap between the depths of the two feelings is unfathomable. And that makes perfect sense. Ignoring this gap, as rationalism does, is what makes no sense. On that point, it is Marglit's argument that seems most persuasive.

THE DIFFERENCE OF THE UNBORN AND THE DEAD

Karatani also speaks about the importance of the relationship with the dead. On this point, I am in complete agreement:

> We cannot even dialogue with the dead or the unborn. We cannot, by any means, undermine the asymmetry of our relationship with them. In that sense, it is they who should, most prototypically, be called "other."[22]

However, there is something I find somewhat problematic with his theory. Can we really take up "the dead" and "the unborn" in the same way? The dead have proper names, have individuality. Although the

22. Karatani, *Ethics 21*, 121.

dead may be buried in the depths of history, with even their names forgotten, it does not change the fact that they were once individual people, living in this world, who then passed away. Also, as is the case with the death of a loved one, it is possible to have a "thick relationship" with a particular deceased person.

In contrast, "the unborn" do not have particular individuality and cannot even be given names (with the exception of fetuses already conceived but yet unborn). Therefore, they cannot form concrete thick relations. And because of this, there is an asymmetry between the dead and the unborn, and they cannot be treated as equal. Even when one says "we cannot even dialogue with them," there is a clear difference between the inability to dialogue with the dead and the inability to dialogue with those who have yet to be born. I am not saying that we have no relationship with the unborn. If that were the case, then after I die, what happens to the world next is none of my business. Karatani is right on that point, but at the very least, there is a difference between the past and the future.

So far, I have focused excessively on Karatani's theory. But what I wish to convey is the decisive and towering issue of whether we shall see the ethics and morality of *ningen* in this life as superior, or if we shall acknowledge the issues that are insoluble within the framework of *ningen*. This is a problem that has dragged on since the debates in the Meiji period on "the clash of education and religion" up until the present.

Not presupposing religion

In the considerations above, we see that there are two possibilities in an ethics / morality that is constructed independent from religion. We can have a stance wherein all problems can be solved within rational ethics / morality (Karatani), or a stance that, while emphasizing emotions that cannot be resolved within a rational standpoint alone, refuses to land in the domain of religion (Marglit). In contrast to these thinkers, I have cautiously carried out my inquiry, beginning with our relationship with the dead, without automatically bringing up religion.

I think this is an extremely important point. People who are involved in religion seem like they think that religion is a given and tend not to question their own faith. Perhaps within their group, discussions might go smoothly despite this attitude. But the minute they step outside that circle, things suddenly grind to a halt. We should be thankful for the sermons of priests and pastors, but these alone tend to become a bit too detached from worldly life. If one would rather rest complacently in this state of things, then fine. However, we must bear in mind that one who refuses to question one's own standpoint and refuses to keep re-tempering it, is destined to fall into petrified dogmatism.

In relation to that, another important point is that it is not possible to have only one standpoint as the correct one. I have to seek out for myself the path that works best for me. But I cannot assert that this path is the only right path, and I do not intend to do so. In the region where the dominion of reason fades, one has no choice but to hone one's sensitivities and emotions, and use these as a guiding thread. But whether or not this path is "correct," no one can say.

26

Rethinking Hiroshima and Yasukuni

In Japan, when one brings up the notions of war and religion, one has to wrestle with the problem of Yasukuni Shrine. But when touching upon that subject, the impression I get is that people are concerned with whether or not the Prime Minister will go on an official visit there or not, and how other countries in Asia (particularly China) will respond to it. This treats the problem as if it were merely a problem of political diplomacy. In response to this, there are talks of building a new secular memorial site, in order to avoid complaints every time the Prime Minister visits, and this is seen as a very promising idea. However, although Yasukuni Shrine was accompanied by a very political agenda from the beginning, as a shrine, it is a religious facility and a place where the dead are enshrined. If we forget this perspective, I fear we will lose sight of the essence of the Yasukuni issue.

Yasukuni has its origins in the Shōkonsha (shrine for invoking the dead) which honored the dead from the loyalist army in the Boshin War (1868–1869). In 1879, Yasukuni Shrine was designated as an imperial shrine of special status. Particularly from the Sino-Japanese and Russo-Japanese wars onward, it became closely linked to the military as a place to enshrine the war dead from wars outside Japan, and bore the role of increasing fighting spirit. This fact has received much scrutiny, especially during the Pacific War that resulted in enormous casualties. This peculiar role of the shrine has had a lasting effect even after the war.

In this way, Yasukuni Shrine has been closely linked to war and played a symbolic role for State Shinto. I think that because of this, even in the post-war period, pro-Yasukuni right-wingers and conservatives have clashed with anti-Yasukuni left-wingers and progressives, in a very stereotypical, dualistic, oppositional schema. And this has come at the expense of any creative discourse on the basis of Yasukuni's religious essence. Furthermore, people tend to think that this is a Shinto issue and is of no relevance to Buddhism or other religions. But in truth, things are hardly that simple.

The relationship between Yasukuni Shrine and the dead

The first thing we need to consider is that although Yasukuni is a shrine, it is a completely different, new type of shrine, compared to the older shrines. We must keep in mind that, in ancient times, people did not become kami, and so nobody honored the dead in shrines. The practice of enshrining the dead as kami began in the early Heian period (794–1185), on the basis of the belief in spirits of the dead. It was believed that people who met untimely deaths due to political conspiracies would die bearing a deep grudge, and thus bring about plagues and other natural disasters after their deaths. In order to appease them, they were enshrined as kami. One archetypical example of this is Kitano Tenmangū (in Kyoto) that enshrines Sugawara no Michizane, as part of *tenjin shinkō*, belief in the spirit of Sugawara no Michizane.

After that, a new type of shrine arose at the beginning of the premodern period that enshrined people as kami. Toyotomi Hideyoshi is enshrined at Toyokuni Shrine, Tokugawa Ieyasu is at Tōshōgū Shrine—we see here that political authorities are deified as kami. This practice preserves the political power of influential people even after their passing, thus supporting the continued prosperity and influence of their descendants. This is completely different from the faith in the spirits of the dead. But it has been noted that *both* the faith in the spirits of the dead and the shrines that deify political figures have a considerable Shinto-Buddhist syncretic character.

However, Yasukuni Shrine has a different character from these shrines of the past. In the case of Yasukuni, it is war dead who are enshrined as kami. Certainly, they lost their lives in an unnatural fashion due to war, and there are many of them who probably died feeling resentful. This shrine was also built with a political intent and is thus similar to shrines that deify political authorities. However, despite these similar elements, those enshrined at Yasukuni are ordinary citizens and not special spirits or political authorities. Also, it is only in this shrine that there are more than 2,466,000 enshrined kami—something unthinkable for other shrines.

Because Yasukuni Shrine deifies dead common folk (although this is restricted to war dead), it takes up the role played by funeral Buddhism. Although Shinto originally lacked funeral rites, in the Edo period, they tried to come up with their own rites and popularized it, in order to depose Buddhism and come into their own as a religion. These were called Shinto funerals, and even contemporary Shinto-style funerals come from this sort of background.

Originally, it was Buddhism that had the deepest relationship with the dead. But when Buddhism tried to modernize and forget the dead, hiding this relationship as if it were something to be ashamed of, it was Shinto that actively strove to build a new relationship with the departed. Today, in Yasukuni Shrine, they have included Bon festival dances during the festival for appeasing the spirits of the dead (*mitama matsuri*), and are taking positive steps to construct novel ways of relating with the deceased.

Furthermore, while Buddhism blatantly discriminates based on how much one pays for a posthumous Buddhist name, everyone is equal at a Shinto shrine. Even in Yasukuni Shrine, privates and generals are enshrined in the same way. From this logic, it makes sense that even Class-A War Criminals are not subjected to any discrimination. As Prime Minister Koizumi put it, "when anyone dies, he or she becomes a buddha." Although he may have mixed up kami and buddhas, I think his basic approach is correct.

I often come across the argument that Yasukuni Shrine only deifies the government forces and those who died for Japan in war, and is thus prejudiced and unequal. However, within the grounds, there is a sub-shrine called Chinreisha (shrine for appeasing the spirits), a new section built in 1965. In this section, the spirits of all those who die in war anywhere in the world are enshrined. If we emphasize the role of Chinreisha, there is a possibility of revising the character of Yasukuni Shrine itself.

Therefore, the idea of "Yasukuni Shrine" changes through history, and is not something that can be settled by a dogmatic yes or no. There is something in this for Buddhists to learn. I think it is necessary for Buddhists not to turn their backs on this as another religion's problem, but rather, relate with it and actively engage with it in a dialogue that aims toward a vision of the future.

NON-SECTARIAN RITES FOR THE CASUALTIES OF THE ATOMIC BOMBS

In contrast to Yasukuni Shrine, which directly involves Shinto, the rites to honor the dead from the atomic bombing are conducted in a non-sectarian manner. We see a different case in Nagasaki, which was originally a place where Christians were persecuted. The relationship with Christianity is very strong here, and we see this in the fact that Urakami Cathedral became the symbol of the bombing of Nagasaki. Soon after the bombing, Nagai Takashi argued that the bombing of Nagasaki was by divine providence, and that those who died were sacrificial lambs laid on the altar of God. This was called the Nagasaki burnt sacrifice view, which was strongly criticized. While it had its problems, the important point that deserves recognition is that it tried to make sense of the atomic bombing from a Christian point of view, starting off that discourse.

In contrast, Hiroshima always had a strong Buddhist foundation—the Followers of Aki (an old name for Hiroshima)—and Buddhism has been considerably involved in comforting the spirits of the dead from disasters. But despite those elements, Buddhism was never able to come to the fore with the Hiroshima peace movement. The public stance has always been a non-sectarian anti-nuclear political peace movement. While this has, as a matter of fact, played an important role, one must consider that it has also become a ground for political disputes and there are downsides to this political involvement. Furthermore, given that today, the political peace movement is reaching its limits, if things remain as they are with Hiroshima, the experience of having been atomic bombed is in real danger of slowly disappearing into irrelevance.

As I have previously mentioned, it is necessary for us at the present to humbly reflect on the possibility that the peace movement had within it a sense of arrogant delusion, wherein peace would be constructed by the power of the living alone, and the dead would merely be people from the past who we want to rest in peace. While people have finally begun to reconsider the role played by Buddhism in comforting the spirits of the dead in Hiroshima, thanks to James Foard's research and Nitta Mitsuko's recently published book *The Atom Bomb and Buddhist Temples*,[23] there is still a long way to go.

When one stands before the memorial stone for the victims of the atomic bomb (the symbol at the center of the Hiroshima Peace Park), one does not necessarily get the feel, the atmosphere, necessary to speak, in silence, with the dead. I hear that instead, the bereaved of the victims pay their respects at the atomic bomb memorial tower, where the ashes of the victims are stored. Despite the importance of the exhibits of the Hiroshima Peace Memorial Museum, it does not provide a space to commune with the dead. If I may speak from my own

---

23. Nitta Mitsuko 新田光子『原爆と寺院』[The atom bomb and Buddhist temples] (Kyoto: Hōzōkan, 2004).

experience, although I hear there were problems with the establishment of the Hiroshima National Peace Memorial Hall for the Atomic Bomb Victims, the empty space in the basement called the memorial space is an excellent place for the past and present to meet, through silent meditation.

What we need to learn from yasukuni

In 2004, there was a film called *Chichi to kuraseba*, renamed in English as "The Face of Jizo," originally by Inoue Hisashi, directed by Kuroki Kazuo. Its plot revolves around a father who died in the atomic bombing but returns as a ghost and tries to encourage his daughter who is plagued by feelings of survivor guilt. In this movie, rather than formalistic pacifism, the question of what can be constructed from the dialogue with the dead finally becomes the main concern. I think this is quite promising.

More than in Hiroshima, it is in Yasukuni where the idea of us in dialogue with the dead and seeking help from the dead (in order to make it into the energy of the living), is progressing. Should we not learn from what ought to be learned, transcending differences of ideology or religion?

Those who died in battle probably had some sort of resolve, despite the fact that they were drafted. However, in Hiroshima, innocent non-combatants, including young children, completely unarmed, were handed the cruelest deaths without any warning. And those who lived had to suffer the rages of radiation poisoning. Their *han* (resentment) is in some way, surely far greater than those enshrined at Yasukuni. Things would definitely improve if the dead in Hiroshima could, so to speak, stand up uncovering, lend a hand to the living, and walk alongside them. Is it not our given duty as the living to make such a space, and to open the way to that possibility?

27

Reconsidering Courtesy to the Dead

Yanagita Kunio's *Tales of the Ancestors* was written in 1945, right before Japan's defeat, and was published right after the end of the war. Foreseeing the abrupt changes of Japanese society, it was written with the aim of documenting the Japanese traditional views of the ancestors and the dead, which are founded on the system of the household (*ie*).

According to Yanagita, there are four points that are peculiar to the view of death in Japan:

> First, [Japanese people] thought that even though one dies, the soul stays within this country and does not go far. Second, they thought that there is a rich interchange between the two worlds—the world of that which is manifest and the world of that which is secluded.[24] This interchange is not restricted merely to regular festivals in spring and autumn, but rather, if one side willed it, it would not be difficult to invite or be invited by the other side. Third, they thought that the deepest desires held by the living at the moment of death would necessarily be fulfilled after death. Fourth, because of this, many thought that not only did people make plans for their descendants, they were reborn over and over again in order to continue these projects.[25]

In other words, there was a way of thinking wherein, as a whole, the worlds of the dead and the living were not far apart but were relatively close to, and interacted with, each other. Even in the present,

24. 顕幽二界.
25. Yanagita Kunio 柳田国男「六四・死の親しさ」[The intimacy of death].

despite the changing of the times and the great transformations of society, there are still ways in which this way of thinking lives on.

Yanagita examines the changes of the events in a Bon festival, and notes that there are various types of what we consider in Japan as "the deceased." The first type includes new spirits of those who have recently passed away. The second includes those who, with the passing of time, have lost their individuality and have become united with the ancestors. The third refers to souls that wander because they have no descendants who worship them. He says that depending on the nature of these souls, the way of worshipping them differs.

Of these types, the third type is becoming a very big problem today, with the dead from events like war and great natural disasters. Furthermore, with the decline in birthrates, a continued line of descent is no longer a given, and the third type of dead is becoming more and more common. The view of the dead presented by Yanagita, which presumed the continuity of the house, needs to change. Considering this, the way of thinking about the first and second types of the dead as ancestors of a single house is also becoming difficult to maintain. Notwithstanding, the question remains as to whether or not the dead have individuality or if they fuse into a collective.

In *Death and Madness*, Watanabe Tetsuo writes that the dead who have individuality are the "face" of the "collective" dead. We can remember concretely the people we love who have passed away. However, in the background of each particular departed person is the expanse of the world of the dead that originates in the infinite past. This cannot be thought of through the notion of individuality. The question of the "face" is taken up in Levinas' idea of the other. But by bringing up the problem of the dead, Watanabe brings this discourse a step further.

THE AMBIGUOUS VIEW OF THE DEAD
IN JAPANESE BUDDHISM

Because Yanagita focused so much on clarifying how people in Japan thought about their ancestors *prior* to the influence of Buddhism, he had a very negative view of Buddhism. He thought that words like "Bon" and "*Hotoke*" (Buddha/s) were originally not Buddhist but had a folk origin. He tried to prove this point, but it was quite impossible to do. A considerable part of the Japanese folkways developed in relation to Buddhism, and it is difficult to separate the two. The ancestor worship Yanagita talks about was, in actuality, greatly shaped by funeral Buddhism.

One must note that in this case, what I refer to as "Buddhism" is not a dogmatically fixed Buddhist doctrine, but rather the Buddhism that has changed and assimilated into Japanese folk customs. Both developed in admixture with each other. Just as there is no such thing as pure Japanese folk customs independent from Buddhism, there is also no such thing as pure Buddhism clearly separated from folkways. Therefore, the Buddhist view of death in Japan is not necessarily the same as that in India or China. But I do not think we should think of it as "impure" or "errant" just because of that.

While it may seem as if the Japanese Buddhist view of the dead varies from sect to sect, these differences are not all that large. Most sects take the standpoint of attaining Buddhahood in this body/life (*sokushin jōbutsu*), and see the dead as immediately becoming buddhas. It may seem as if the Pure Land line is an exception, but as the True Pure Land school takes the view that "passing to the next life, as it is, is *nirvāṇa*," it is therefore not too far from *sokushin jōbutsu*. Only the Pure Land school of Hōnen takes the stance, at least officially, that after death, one carries out further Buddhist spiritual practices in the Pure Land.

While the formalities of funeral services are organized in a very systematic fashion in each school, the view of the dead is not as clear. Most sects advocate attaining Buddhahood in this life, but at the same time see the next life in a way similar to the Pure Land, and these two views overlap. Furthermore, while one may become a *Hotoke* as per the *sokushin jōbutsu* view, it is not clear if this is equivalent to Buddha's attainment of final *nirvāṇa*. Furthermore, if the dead had attained *nirvāṇa*, they ought to all be equal. If so, it is not clear what would happen to the individuality of the dead. If the dead become buddhas, it should be the dead who save the living. But why do the living have to give prayers for the repose of the souls of the dead? It makes no sense. Additionally, if the dead all pass to the next life and become buddhas, there would be no point in expounding the theory of *saṃsāra*. But the fact is that this view of *saṃsāra* still remains.

As we see, the views of the dead in Japanese Buddhism are rather confused. While Tibetan Buddhism has spelled out a clear view of the afterlife, as seen in *The Tibetan Book of the Dead*, I find it very strange that Japanese Buddhism, which is called funeral Buddhism, is the one that is unclear about it. Perhaps this is because, despite its name, "funeral Buddhism" has not really emphasized funerals by giving it a central place in the core of their philosophies. Rather, funerals have been treated in a rather careless way, and have not been given sufficient consideration in doctrinal and philosophical discussion.

These issues were put aside by taking the teachings imported from India and China as the outward (*tatemae*) philosophies, but inwardly (*honne*), funeral Buddhism lay concealed. This is very similar to the situation in Japan wherein the *tatemae* was that monks took a stance of a celibate dedication to practice, whereas the *honne* was that in actuality, it was normal for them to take on wives. But the state of things as they are cannot nurture a philosophy original to Japanese Buddhism.

WHY HAVE MODERN BUDDHIST THINKERS DISMISSED FUNERAL BUDDHISM?

However, there were unavoidable circumstances that led to this. With the coming of modernity, the modernist rationalism of the west flooded into Japan, and faced by this immense pressure, Japanese traditional thought and religion were forced to transform considerably. There was a demand to reorganize Buddhism as a religion for the living in *this* world (or *this* life, as opposed to the *other*/*after*life), rather than as funeral Buddhism. For the Buddhist thinkers who represented modernity, the greatest task was how to reinterpret Buddhism as a philosophy and religion for the present life. Furthermore, with the separation of Buddhism and Shinto, the Buddhist side considered the influence of indigenous folk customs of Japan on Buddhism as an embarrassment, and rushed to construct a pure Buddhist philosophy purged of these ambiguities.

An example of this is Kiyozawa Manshi, who recast Pure Land Buddhism not as a religion for the dead but rather as the direct relationship between the absolute infinite being, Tathāgata, and human beings. Another example is D. T. Suzuki, who cast out antiquated temple Zen, and tried to purify Zen as a Zen for laypersons. Also, we have the Nichirenist, Tanaka Chigaku, who after returning to secular life, tried to construct a new Buddhism founded on the household. In this way, radical modern Buddhist thinkers cast out funeral Buddhism and tried to rethink Buddhism as a rational philosophy for this life. Elements colored by esoteric Buddhism (which contains an irrational ambiguity) were rejected, alongside the syncretism of Shinto and Buddhism, as premodern. These would only return after the 1980s.

Of course, I have no intention of denying the efforts of those who struggled throughout modernity. For these thinkers, Buddhism was first resurrected as modern philosophy. But at the same time, would it not be a betrayal of those who tried to revive Buddhism as a contemporary concern, to close our eyes to the limits of modernity that are seen today? It is only by critically overcoming these limitations that we can truly inherit their spirit.

BRINGING BACK COEXISTENCE WITH THE DEAD
FROM THE STANDPOINT OF JAPANESE BUDDHISM

The modern Japanese (intellectual) rejection of funeral Buddhism is connected to the fact that western modern philosophy is founded on an arrogance of the living that ignores death and the dying. Scientific rationalism scoffed at the previous view of the afterlife as irrational and unscientific. This rationalism developed toward materialism (as opposed to idealism), which, together with nihilism, is often seen as a negation of God. But it must be said that the negation of the dead is even prior to the negation of God. As the power of the dead comes to be belittled, as people lose touch with their capacity for speaking with the dead, and as the living begin to pride themselves in that which the dead have given them, as if they had taken these by their own hands, the arrogance of the living grows to an extreme, unchecked, quickly pushing them toward their own downfall.

The people called "Japanese philosophers" often simply copy westerners, imitating Heidegger and prattling about the forgetfulness of Being and nihilism. But I have doubts as to the extent that they philosophize on the basis of the actual circumstances in Japan. More than the forgetfulness of Being, it is the forgetfulness of the dead that is a serious problem. In Japan, it is necessary for us to be able to have a firm footing in our own tradition and theorize from there, rather than go imitating people indiscriminately like monkeys.

Fortunately, although funeral Buddhism has been reduced to a mere shell, Japan still has the *potential* to dialogue with the dead on the basis of this Buddhism. Furthermore, the view of the dead is in the very foundations of Mahāyāna Buddhism, as we see in *The Lotus Sutra*. Pure Land Buddhism too was originally a religion of the dead. From the standpoint of Japanese Buddhism, there is sufficient potential to restore our coexistence with the dead and develop a new philosophy.

Today, the ethics established within the "betweenness of persons" is reaching a point of collapse. The view that ethics reigns supreme, which tries to think of things only from the point of view of the world of the living, is a mistake. It is necessary for us to go beyond ethics and morality and take the standpoint of trans-ethics. We are called to take our point of departure from a face-to-face encounter with the other and the dead, who deviate from inter-personal ethics and are irreducible to it. Having our existence fundamentally shaken in this encounter, we are called to thoroughly reckon with the fragility of the living.

28

Reconstructing Religion from the Dead

Up until this point, I have argued that there are problems that cannot be grasped from within a strictly inter-personal ethics, and that they have to be reconsidered from a dimension that transcends that. In order to discuss these, I have taken the standpoint of our relationship with the dead. Even a philosophical materialist would have to admit the reality of our relationship with the dead, and in that sense this discussion can stand even without presupposing religion. The dead are near to the domain of *ningen*, and though they may not enter that domain, it is possible to give structure to the world of the dead to the extent that they lie at the margins.

However, if one tries to go even beyond the realm of the dead and step far beyond the human realm, common understanding and theoretical pursuits become impossible. When one goes beyond the domain of *ningen*, one can no longer express things through rational words, and one must commit the performative contradiction of speaking the *unspeakable*. But is that even possible?

Certainly if we examine history, we find various religions, each having formed extremely detailed theories. Particularly in the west, there has been a strict delineation between philosophy, which can be elucidated rationally, and theology, which transcends the former. In comparison, Asian traditions have not necessarily established a clear delineation between the two. Certain aspects of this ambiguity are acceptable, but we need to sufficiently reconsider the parts where this causes important problems to become vague and only superficial aspects to be made theoretically consistent.

Definitely, today it is no longer possible to cleanly delineate between philosophy and theology as it was done back when Christianity was the dominant religion. However, it is clear that we cannot deal with the problems that can be spoken of with the words of *ningen* on the same level as the problems that go beyond that domain, which necessitate daring to speak the unspeakable. Imamura Hitoshi wrote a book, *Kiyozawa Manshi and Philosophy*[26] that presents an interpretation of Buddhism that is worth paying attention to. He refers to the Buddhist discourse that tries to speak the unspeakable "Buddhology" (*Buddagaku*, as distinguished from Buddhist studies, *Bukkyōgaku*), which is analogous to theology.

From his early work, *The Skeleton of Religious Philosophy*, up until the last years when he advocated his spiritualism, Kiyozawa Manshi rarely used proper nouns like Amitābha. Rather, he used general designations like infinite (being) or absolute infinite (being), and tried to clarify the problem of religion as concerned with the relationship between us finite beings and the infinite. Imamura follows the same methodology. In his work, the equivalent of the infinite is "Buddha." However, the absolute infinite is on a different plane as us finite beings, and we cannot completely understand the absolute. We finite beings merely grasp the infinite in proportion to our abilities. Finite beings imagine the infinite in their own image, and because of this, Imamura says that such an infinite is a sort of metaphor, an anthropomorphization.

THE PARADOX OF THE ABSOLUTE BEING

However, there is quite a conundrum within this problem. If the infinite being as we understand it is but a metaphor or anthropomorphization of the real infinite being, how can we verify if such meta-

26. Imamura Hitoshi 今村仁司『清沢満之と哲学』[Kiyozawa Manshi and philosophy] (Tokyo: Iwanami Shoten, 2004).

phors or anthropomorphizations are appropriate or not? If the infinite being were really an absolute infinite being, there would be a gap completely separating the infinite from the finite, and even metaphorically, it ought to transcend the understanding of finite beings. It is not possible for such an infinite being to have a relationship with finite beings, who are of a different scale. The very notion of the infinite being having a relationship with finite beings is a contradictory utterance—and we are compelled to accept that contradiction.

This paradox of the absolute infinite being is addressed most directly in the *Old Testament*, far more than it is in Buddhist scriptures. While the God of the *Old Testament* bestowed blessings upon the Israelites, it was hard to know ultimately what was intended by these. When Abraham finally had a child in his old age, a son Isaac, God asked Abraham to sacrifice Isaac. Also, God made Job, who was known as a pious man, undergo all sorts of suffering in order to test his faith. Why does God put particular people, usually very faithful people, through these trials? Why are others able to get by without having to undergo such trials? No matter what, God's will goes beyond the understanding of finite human beings. The more we try to understand him, the further God slips from our grasp.

No matter how we think, our thoughts are finite, and there is certainly something that exceeds the bounds of thought. The more we think, the further we get from the infinite. Contemporary philosophy calls this "that which cannot be manifest" or "the concealed." The God of the *Old Testament*, who is the extreme form of this, transcends the opposition between theism and atheism, between existence and non-existence; God is beyond this world itself, but at the same time, is someone who supports this world.

The turn to Christianity and the construction of the idea of the Christ as mediator was in part due to the inability to bear this sort of paradox of the infinite being. Through Jesus Christ, who is both God and human, the space of absolute separation between the infinite being (God) and finite beings (humans) was bridged, and for the first time, both sides could be reconciled. However, the introduction of such a mediator can dilute the awe felt by us finite beings toward something that we can never understand.

BUDDHA EXISTS ONLY IN RELATION WITH THE FINITE

One does not see this rigid separation between the infinite and the finite in Buddhism. A buddha may have an immense amount of power, but originally, such a buddha was still originally a person who realized enlightenment, and is thus qualitatively the same as a person. In Chapter 7, I brought up the problem of Buddha-nature, and that concept points to none other than the qualitative sameness between the Buddha and the self. It is due to the presence of this sameness that buddhas can save people and that people can depend on buddhas. This is most appropriately expressed in the Tendai theory of the mutual containment of the ten realms: The ten realms of the hell-beings, hungry ghosts, animals, *asura*, humans, gods, *śrāvaka*, *pratyekabuddha*, bodhisattva, and buddhas all mutually subsume each other. And so the realm of the buddhas includes elements of hell, and hell includes elements of the Buddha realm as well.

If this is the case, then a buddha's existence is also finite. On one hand, Kiyozawa Manshi sets up the Buddha as the absolute infinite being, but on the other hand, he asserts that Buddha only exists in relating to us, and that Buddha does not exist in itself. "It is not that we believe in kami and buddhas because they exist, but rather, kami and buddhas exist for us because we believe."[27] If buddhas can only exist within a relationship with finite beings, then buddhas are nothing more than finite existents.[28]

27. Kiyozawa Manshi: 「宗教は主観的事実なり」[Religion is a subjective fact].

28. [As Japanese does not distinguish between "a buddha" and "buddhas," it is difficult to tell when Kiyozawa is referring to them in the singular and the plural. When he stresses the Buddha/s as the absolute infinite being, it makes sense to have it in the singular. But when he refers to *shinbutsu* (kami and buddhas), it is clearly plural. This issue

I would like to draw attention to how we Japanese often call the dead "*Hotoke*" or "*Hotoke-sama*." This is by no means a mere metaphor or popular misunderstanding. The dead are the other whom we are forced to encounter in the margins of the world of *ningen*. The dead are no longer within this human realm, but despite that, we are still compelled to relate with them. People say that death is the completion of life, but it is not that simple. The dead as other is not necessarily friendly to us. On the one hand, they can look out for us, but on the other, they are always unpredictable, uncanny beings from a parallel world. We need to relate with the dead with a sense of discretion and awe.

As I have mentioned previously in relation to *The Lotus Sutra*, the other that draws near in this manner is none other than a buddha. If so, it makes sense that the dead, the most other of others, are referred to as buddhas. If the dead are buddhas, the living who can approach the dead directly must also be buddhas.

As the ideas of attaining buddhahood in this body (*sokushin jōbutsu*) and sudden enlightenment suggest, there is no buddha separate from this body. If the being that must relate with the other is a bodhisattva, and the other that one relates with is a buddha, then the I that can truly approach the other (Buddha) must also be a buddha. In *The Lotus Sutra*, it says, "None but a buddha, together with a buddha, can fully preach and understand the truth well."[29] *The Lotus Sutra* can only be understood by buddhas. The fact that Buddha preached it to us means the recognition that we are also buddhas. Anyone who can enter the world of *The Lotus Sutra* is none other than a buddha.

---

reveals certain limitations in Kiyozawa's attempt to reframe Buddhism according to the model of monotheistic religions.]

29. 唯仏与仏乃能究尽.

TRANSCENDING THIS-WORLD-ISM

However, can I become a buddha completely? In actuality, it is not easy to truly face the other / dead and live in response to their power. There is a danger that the power of the dead might overwhelm the living, go beyond our control, and oppose us. We need an even greater power to govern the dead, and that is none other than the power of buddhas.

As I have mentioned in Chapter 21, in *The Lotus Sutra*, Buddha acquired his great power through his relationship with the dead Prabhūtaratna Tathāgata. Buddha has always had a deep relationship with the dead. While Buddha's *nirvāṇa* is ultimate enlightenment, it is also death. By Buddha's becoming a dead person, he attained his authentic power as a buddha. Buddhist interpretations of *nirvāṇa* are divided into various theories, and in some cases, *nirvāṇa* is misunderstood as a nihilism where one returns to nothingness. However, what is most important here is the paradoxical situation, that death is enlightenment, and death is the only way to become a true buddha.

When it comes to this deep relationship with the dead, buddhas are very different from the kami of Japan. Buddhas relate with the dead, and through that relationship come to relate with the living. But with growing rationalization and this-worldliness, the relationship with the dead tends to fall into neglect. Although in actuality, it is funeral Buddhism that is taken as foundational, it does not receive sufficiently deep reflection as the starting point of Buddhism. Theoretically, this attitude can be referred to as "this-world-ism."

Modern Buddhist leaders, including Kiyozawa Manshi and Tanaka Chigaku, took back Buddhism from the yonder shore and reconstructed it as a religion for us people living in this world. Their efforts are very important, and one should not make light of these. However, in the present, such a this-world-ism has fallen into an impasse, and we need to turn once more to a close examination of the relationship with the dead in Buddhism.

29

Where Does One Go after Death?

Usually, a person's own death is taken as the greatest issue for religion. In contrast to that, I think that prior to one's own death, we need to first concern ourselves with the problem of the dead as the other that we have no choice but to relate with in actuality. I have suggested shifting the problem from "death" to "the dead." But then, how is one to think about one's own death?

To put it plainly, there is no way for us to know what comes after death. Indeed, we inevitably come into relation with the dead. But despite that, we cannot know what sort of a state the dead are in. That is a matter of fact. This is because the dead are not beings who can be positioned within the time and space of the world of *ningen*, and not to mention, one cannot perceive them with one's senses. At best, we can do no more than speak of them metaphorically.

We know no more than the aspect by which the dead face us. However, come to think of it, it is not just the dead—how well do we know the other? Just because someone is a colleague whom I work with, I do not necessarily know about his private life. Even family members do not entirely understand what the others are thinking deep down inside. To go even further, in truth we do not understand our very own minds and hearts. More so, just how much can we understand about the matters of the dead?

When venturing into uncharted territory, one prepares and gathers information, relying on the words of people who have experience, for example, as to what kind of place it is. However, since unlike the living, the dead cannot speak with the words of *ningen*, we cannot get "information" (in the usual sense) from them.

It is true that since the olden days, people have gone to spirit media or have turned to dreams in order to get information from the dead. Ever since the medieval period in Japan, there have been many records of dreams and auspicious omens indicating that a person had passed on to the Pure Land. However, naturally, this is quite different from verifiable information. Perhaps one can believe in these as individuals. But while things may have been different in the medieval period, today, people are no longer convinced by these. People made a bit of a fuss over "near-death experiences," but these are, after all, near-death, not death.

THE DEAD ARE BUDDHAS, AS AM I

If so, can we believe the words in the scriptures that have been spoken by Buddha? In Buddha's case, one can say that he was also well-versed in the matters of the world of the dead. However, even if that may be so, is it really true that the Pure Land is some *nouveau riche* world with gold gilding and gems all about, as it is written in *The Sūtra of Immeasurable Life*? I do not think one would even hope for such a stuffy world like that. Because of this, the depictions of the Pure Land are usually read as a kind of metaphor, and there have been many varied interpretations of it. We do not have to believe things literally just because the Buddha said so.

If so, does that mean that in the end, one has to take an agnostic stance vis-à-vis what comes after death? To the contrary, one can say that we can hope (*negau*), and we can strive toward that hope. Certainly, we are weak beings who cannot even freely control our own minds and hearts. We do not even know what lies within us. I am an *other* to myself, unfathomable to myself. The consciousness-only theory of Buddhism teaches us that in the deepest parts of our minds, there is a domain completely beyond the grasp of ordinary understanding.

Despite all this, one can hope that things go well. In reality, more than by anyone else, I am betrayed most by myself. Although I may try to live with good intentions, it is impossible to live selflessly with purely good intentions. But still, one can hope for the best. Furthermore, it is impossible that efforts toward such might be completed in this life. The hope that things be well can continue and endure after death, and one can intend a perfection greater that what was achieved within this lifetime. We do not need to look at death as the absolute conclusion, where all things come to an end.

And just as we now relate with the dead, after death, we, as the dead, can watch over the living and relate with them. Or better yet, we ought to relate with them. In the words of Shinran, this is the problem of *gensō*, returning from the Pure Land. Tanabe Hajime took a Zen master's compassion continuing after death as the archetypal example of "existential communion with the dead." One cannot say, "Well I am going to die anyway, so it does not matter what happens to this world." It is precisely because things do not end with death that we must feel a sense of responsibility toward future generations.

If one thinks about it this way, there is no need to take a theory of the eternal life of the soul (as in Christianity) or presuppose an Indian view of transmigration. We do not even know what will happen tomorrow. There is no way we could clearly know about what happened before birth and what will happen after death. If one starts bringing up disconnected and abstract ideas all of a sudden—like eternity and infinity—all it does is stir up an anxiety and fear that one is bluffing.

In this way, the dead are beings we are compelled to relate with in the present. But at the same time, we ourselves will sooner or later enter that world. If so, while the dead are other, of a different nature from the living, simultaneously they are also close to us, of a similar nature, beings whom we have continuity with. The dead are also buddhas, and so are we. We speak with the dead, we live with the dead. This might sound strange to people who cannot see or think of things otherwise than on the plane of *ningen*, but it is a view that many people are actually living out.

THE ROLE OF MONKS IN MEDIATING
THE DEAD AND THE LIVING

Of course there are cases when the dead directly call out to the living, but often, we need a mediating specialist in the relationship between the dead and the living. Sometimes that would be someone like a shaman who calls on the spirits of the dead. But in Japan, it is Buddhist monks who have functioned as the main religious professionals who maintain the order between the dead and the living in a more stable manner. It is because of this that I have repeatedly stressed the importance of funeral Buddhism in this book.

Recently, Ueda Noriyuki, who wrote *Go Buddhism!*,[30] sensed a crisis in this present state of Buddhism. He has placed his hopes for the future of Buddhism in "event monks" who go beyond funeral Buddhism and can conduct their activities in a lively manner. There are parts of this I am sympathetic to, but I think that there is no other way to revive Japanese Buddhism than to thoroughly reconsider its characteristic funeral Buddhism and reconstruct this on a firm philosophical basis.

In the medieval period, it was thought that the dead who had no place to go went everywhere, bringing harm and misfortune to the living. Buddhism began to fulfill its role through through incantations that powerfully confined the wandering dead. But today, things are reversed: It has become difficult to hear the voices of the dead and they tend to be ignored. If so, then we ought to pay respects to the dead, hearken to their call, and construct a system that allows them to coop-

30. Ueda Noriyuki 上田紀行『がんばれ仏教！』[Go Buddhism!] (Tokyo: NHK Bukku-su, 2004).

erate with the living. This is the important role that has been bestowed to Buddhism in Japan today.

RE-TEMPERING FUNERAL BUDDHISM

However, as I have repeatedly been saying, the funeral Buddhism of today will not do. The present funeral Buddhism has degenerated into merely habitual ceremonies, and has turned into no more than an income source for temples. Just how seriously are professional priests thinking about the present situation where people decry "*bōzu marumōke*" (bald priest's profiteering)?

Also, times change. Contemporary funeral Buddhism stands on top of the *ie* (house) system and presupposes that descendants will protect their ancestors' graves. But today, people hardly concern themselves with the continuity of the *ie*. People do not want to be placed within the family graves so we now have graves for couples or individuals. Also, things are no longer restricted to cemeteries attached to temples, and people in big cities seem to like non-sectarian public cemeteries. Not only that, the movement for natural funerals is popular, and such funerals do not require grave sites. Now, people no longer have to adhere to given formats for their own funerals or graves, but can think about it and design it for themselves.

The image of death has also changed. I noticed that lately, people very often refer to the dead as "my dad who went to heaven" or "so-and-so-san in heaven." It is not the Buddhist paradise but rather heaven that is seen as the place where the dead are. Perhaps as Christian weddings have become the most widespread, the Christian image of the world after death is also being taken up, albeit with much Japanizing.

If so, Buddhism can no longer have a monopoly over the dead like it used to. The era when Buddhist temples and priests related with the dead with a special sense of privilege is over. Perhaps from now on, Buddhist temples will be downsized and will pass through "natural selection." The era when the dead were fully entrusted to monks has come and gone. The dead have to relate with all the living, and we ought to bear a degree of responsibility toward our own deaths that is commensurate to that fact.

If this is the case, then Buddhist specialists should also make good use of their past experiences, actively think about how we ought to relate with the dead, and share that with others. Amidst that, funeral Buddhism naturally needs to change. The part of that I cannot help but feel strange about is posthumous Buddhist names (*kaimyō*). Such a name is said to be one's name as a disciple of the Buddha, and is given when one receives the precepts. Receiving the precepts is a form of initiation, and therefore, originally one ought to receive the precepts while alive. But if that did not happen, then after death, a ritual is carried out, and a posthumous Buddhist name is bestowed.

However, to be perfectly honest, that is no more than *tatemae*, a superficial stance. In practice, almost nobody receives the precepts within one's lifetime, and posthumous Buddhist names play the role of what we might call an initiation for the dead, wherein by giving a name to the deceased as one of the dead, he or she is distinguished from the living and sent off to the world of the dead. But why is it that there are distinctions here with regard to the length of the posthumous names or other honorific suffixes? And why is that swayed by the size of the donation? It is preposterous. Buddhists like these would never be able to preach equality. If we are complacent and do not renew our efforts, Buddhism has no other fate than decline.

30

Departing Once Again from the Everyday

As we draw to the end of this book, there are still many problems left undiscussed, and I hope to leave these tasks for another time. To end, I would like to reorganize my fundamental points from a slightly different angle, and supplement things somewhat.

What I wanted to emphasize most in this book is that the public sphere (*Öffentlichkeit*), which we are apt to think of as complete onto itself, is actually not that self-evidently so. Today, people often speak of "public philosophy." Of course, it is necessary to give consideration to the public sphere, and I have no intention of denying that. But if advocates of such a philosophy think that all can be settled merely through the public, that is an outrageous error. Rather, the origin of the various problems of today lies in how the stress on the public sphere tends to omit the problems that dribble out from the edges of public space.

It is true that we live within roles vis-à-vis one another, and this is the way of being of *ningen* that is the "betweenness of persons." Even in the private sphere, which is thought of as the opposite of the public sphere, mutual comprehension exists through inter-personal relations like parent-child, husband-wife, lovers, and friends. Originally, words come into circulation within the public sphere, and if we depart from the realm of the inter-personal, we can no longer rely on words, and discourse becomes impossible.

Nevertheless, we know that there are some things that slip from the grasp of such a public sphere. When one says, "a pain in my heart that no one can understand," some might argue that nobody actually thinks that it is incomprehensible. But surely, this phrase is meaningful, and it can be understood by other people. And so paradoxically, we cannot say "no one can understand" this pain. But despite this, there are situations when we cannot help but say, "a pain in my heart that no one can understand."

For example, when a child who is contemplating suicide laments, "Nobody understands these feelings that are driving me to my death," this cannot make sense within the language of the public sphere. However, if there is a person who has experienced something similar even just once, that person can no longer turn his or her back on those "non-sensical" words.

By no means does this mean that one's previous experience is identical with what this child is going through. That experience belongs to that person alone. In that sense, his words, "nobody understands," are correct. Yes, it is impossible to convey to anyone something that only you understand. There is a contradiction in trying to convey that. If I deign to comprehend the child's feelings, it might just be a presumption on my part, and perhaps the pain this child feels is entirely different. But nevertheless, the suffering within this child's heart haunts me.

One can organize this through the principles of compassion and sympathy and try to find an ethics from there. However, that will not succeed, because how one sympathizes with the child's appeal also varies from person to person and is not something that can be generalized. That might link up to my actions in some way, but my actions will not necessarily be ethical. Rather, if one sympathizes with a person who has deviated from the framework of the "betweenness of persons," that sort of sympathy may be dangerous and inadmissible within the public sphere.

On the other hand, one might bring up the way of thinking that sees the realization of the authentic way of being oneself as something made possible only by transcending this role-based inter-personal realm. For example, Heidegger's philosophy is of this sort. However, is there really such a thing as authenticity (or in Heideggerian parlance, what is "ownmost")? What we encounter in the place beyond the inter-personal is the other—with whom we cannot cope, and whom we cannot manage. The self itself also betrays the grotesque that goes beyond self-control. These are completely different from what glamorous words like "authenticity" indicate. But despite that, we need to relate with this sort of other.

Religion as linking the inter-personal and that which transcends it

The above argument might be countered by saying that going beyond the "betweenness of persons" is a problem for but a few strange people, and is of no concern to the majority. However, somehow I doubt that is the case. I think most people are likely to have experienced irrational feelings that do not stay within the confines of public rules: Jealousy, hate, desire for the opposite sex—things that if we spoke about or acted on them, we would end up sexually harassing someone or committing a crime. There is nobody who has never experienced stirrings like these. If someone said he had never experienced anything of this sort, then rather than being a sage, what is more likely is that he/she has actually experienced these but repressed it, and is fooling him/herself into thinking otherwise. That would be even more dangerous.

As the utmost limit of the other who does not abide by public, inter-personal rules, we have the dead. The dead never enter the "betweenness of persons." We cannot call the dead to a meeting table and argue with them. But nevertheless, a person who has experienced the death of someone close probably knows that the dead do not cease to exist due to their dying. Rather, because of their passing, they can urge us more forcefully than the living, and they do not leave us be.

Religion, to put it concisely, is what is constituted in the place that binds in a tensional relationship both the inter-personal and that which transcends the inter-personal. It teaches what deviates toward the world beyond the inter-personal, from within the inter-personal.

But at the same time, religion does not remain within this deviation, but rather tries to retrieve the inter-personal. It is in the tensional relationship in the boundaries of both domains that religion comes to be. Unlike science, law, ethics, and the like, which, although they may seem to deal with deviations, always reduce these to the "between-ness of persons," religion does not take this one-sided path. And it is because of this that religion itself can give rise to deviance, and has the power to stir up violence and crime.

In Japan, when one speaks of *shūkyō* (religion), it is often thought of with a very peculiar nuance. New religions and Christianity are considered to be the prototypical religions, and religions tend to be thought of as insular groups bound by strong faith, and populated by social outcasts—dangerous people even. It is as if religion is automatically equated to something like a cult. Because of this, most Japanese declare themselves to be *mushūkyō* (not having a religion).

Within this state of affairs is the following consideration: When the concept of *shūkyō* was popularized as the translation of "religion," it was accompanied by a nuance of the superiority of Christianity. Because of this, religion was understood with a Christian prototype of the relationship with an absolute being (God). Thus things like Japan's syncretism of Shinto and Buddhism were considered to be something uncivilized and of a low level. Buddhism also devised a theoretical construction modeled after Christianity, but things like funeral Buddhism and the syncretism of Shinto and Buddhism, which did not fit within that framework, were covered over. The discourse that Shinto is not a religion ended up strengthening the restrictions of this conception of religion even more, and religion could not be thought of otherwise from this very particular and limited manner.

Furthermore, this sort of belittling of religion was spurred on, this time by modern rationalism, which saw religion as something premodern. The scientism and Darwinism of the 19th century looked down on irrational religion and considered it necessary to replace it with rational ethics. In the postwar period, these were quickened by the flourishing of the social sciences and materialism. Marxism saw religion as an opium and attacked it, and the influence of modernists like Max Weber ended up criticizing non-protestant religions as unfit for modernity.

THAT WHICH SUPPORTS OUR LIVES

Today, the redefinition of "religion" has become an issue for scholars of religious studies. However, no matter how one may define religion, so long as it is an issue of the definition of a scholarly field, it will remain fundamentally unable to transcend the domain of *ningen*. "Religious studies" as a study is possible only by considering religion as a phenomenon within the framework of *ningen*. Therefore, religious studies can never grasp the most fundamental task of religion—the relationship with the dimension that transcends *ningen*. This is the basic dilemma of the "study" called "religious studies."

If we look at religion as the relationship with the realm that transcends the human, then it is not a special phenomenon, but rather it becomes a problem that involves almost all people. For example, even if one hates Buddhist funerals and adopts "secular" funerals, so long as one does not deal with this by throwing out corpses like trash, then one remains connected in some way to this relationship with the dead, and one cannot help but engage a problem irreducible to the domain of *ningen*.

This is very different from the preexisting definitions of "religion," and if one would argue that we ought to use a different name to designate it, I do not think we need to be attached to the word "religion" or "*shūkyō*." However, when it comes to this problem, it is religion that has most deeply related to it ever since. Because of this, I think there is no harm in using the designation "religion."

I think we are too caught up in a restricted form of common sense. Because of this, the mere mention of the idea of deviating from the realm of *ningen*, can itself draw spite and suspicion. However, it should not be this way. If we look back on our own selves in a more honest way, we find that we are always relating with something that transcends the domain of the human. I think it would be good to take this fact as our point of departure. If one sets aside the fetters of common sense and fixes one's eyes upon him/herself, then perhaps one will know that what lies in the place beyond the realm of *ningen* is not just grotesque things, things to be disgusted by, but the very things which support our lives and give us courage. It is not that there is anything special when one says "trans-ethics"—it is no different from how things are in our everyday lives.

Afterword

For almost 30 years, I had devoted myself solely to the basic task of constructing a history of thought on the basis of Buddhist classical texts. For a person like me who tends to be withdrawn and to have a tough time with interpersonal relations, this job was my vocation. However, since a few years ago, I started working with researchers from philosophy, ethics, and other cutting-edge contemporary fields in things like collaborative research projects. But it was hard to keep up with their discussions, and I often felt out of place. As a mere intellectual artisan, I am not fond of the complexities of the world, and I have scraped by, bit by bit, relying only on the meager skill of dealing with texts. The brilliant arguments of "intellectuals" debating exhaustively about the state of the world seemed to be of another dimension, and I always felt stumped. The state of the world? I could not even figure out how to live my own life. And so I wandered aimlessly about.

However, if that is how I am, then I have nowhere else to start from except this self, pathetic though it may be. What can I do to most frankly express my feelings and thoughts just as they are? And thus began my quest, my groping in the dark. In the midst of the thinking that formed the motifs of this book—my doubt as to whether public ethics was really as foundational as it is said to be or not, the difficulty of relating with the other, and my relative sense of closeness to the dead—I looked within myself, and in dialogue with myself, things slowly took shape. Since, unlike other philosophers and ethicists, I lack training in western thought, I relied on what knowledge I had of Buddhism, which I feel some kinship with. However, these were not merely borrowed philosophies for me. Perhaps this may be conceited, but I wanted to think from the tradition that I myself had received.

Thus I went by way of trial and error. But my faltering words were far too removed from common sense, such that when I spoke with others, I often got this face as if to say "you're making no sense whatsoever." Sometimes, I got a sneer, or even got told off. And so I never managed to have any confidence in my own philosophy, and I fell into anguish, hesitating to express my thoughts. But during this time, I read the works of Watanabe Tetsuo and the philosophy of Tanabe Hajime, both of whom dealt directly with our relationship with the dead. My encounter with them gave me a good deal of courage. And I started to wonder if maybe my way of thinking had not been altogether misguided.

Right at that time, I got a call from Yazawa Chōdō of Kōzansha Publishing, asking me if I could write a serial for the monthly magazine *The Prosperity of Temples*, an industry magazine aimed at those who work in temples. Until today, I do not quite understand why they would have asked this from someone like me. But it was great timing, and so I agreed, thinking that this would be a good chance to boldly express myself in writing, while at the same time organizing my own ideas. That serial publication was entitled "Lectures on Buddhist Trans-Ethics/Morality" and ran 30 issues from the January 2003 issue to the one in June 2005.

It is but a minor magazine that is not widely known. But unexpectedly, the serial had readers. And so this time around, I was invited by Masuda Kenji of Chikuma Shobō to write a book based on the contents of the serial. This being the case, I thought that rather than a newly written text, I could just take things easy by editing and consolidating the serialized lectures. And so I got to work—and my bright prospects quickly turned to regret. I added an extra chapter, reordered things, revised everything, and at the end of the day, it took almost as much time and effort as writing it from scratch. Every time I felt like throwing the manuscript out, Masuda severely reprimanded me like an *oni*, and we passed the draft back and forth as much as five times before it took the form of a proper new book. Because of this, Yazawa and Masuda are the real "parents" of this book.

When it came to deciding on the name of the book, the headaches began anew. Masuda and I had endless discussions, and then disagreements came from the Sales Department. Shortly before the deadline, the idea came up: *Buddhism vs. Ethics*. We were worried that this name might draw the ire of "serious" researchers, but I hope people will understand that this title somewhat playfully expresses the tensional relationship between the trans-ethics of "Buddhism" (or more broadly, "religion") and "ethics."

Because I was fumbling about, there may be things that I have not given sufficient consideration to, despite their being important problems. For example, I think that the problems of gender, including the problems of sexual minorities, are fundamental when thinking about the other. But I did not get to take this up in this book. I leave these issues for another time.

January 2006

Appendix

The Horizon of the Theory of the Other and the Dead

This book was first published in Japan in 2006, but the journal serial publication was from 2003 to 2005. This book represents one great period for me. I would like to start by first writing about the chronology leading up to the publication of this book.

In the afterword of the Shinsho edition (the first edition) of this book, I wrote, "For almost 30 years, I devoted myself solely to the simple task of constructing a history of thought on the basis of classical Buddhist texts. For a person like me who tends to be withdrawn and have a tough time with interpersonal relations, this job was my vocation." I explained this with a bit more detail in the afterword of my book *Dismantling Words and Worlds*.[1] Please do forgive the long quote:

> When I was young, I aspired toward philosophy but met with no success. I got into literature, but that failed. I sought out religion, but I was set back there as well. Floundering at everything, I grew cowardly and desperately shut myself up within my shell. I turned my back on the spirit of the times, and lost all interest in social affairs. It was only the texts from a distant and forgotten past that gave me certain consolation—these were friends that would never betray me. Going through the characters bestowed traces, the world of the past unexpectedly spread forth before me, and I was intoxicated. And so I entered the

1. 『解体する言葉と世界』 [Dismantling words and worlds] (Tokyo: Iwanami Shoten, 1998).

world of philology. It was a sort of fanatic, *otaku* world, and it would be maddeningly boring, surely unbearably meaningless, for anyone who lacked that interest. But it fit me. Perhaps, in truth, it is something that does neither harm nor good, but in my case, it was my guilty pleasure.

Philology (although I think this may be true for other disciplines) is not an expression of some noble spirit to the degree that people think. It is simple, and is carried out by acquiring and applying techniques that are almost the same as an artisan's skills. Even though seemingly novel theories may come out in droves, they are applicable to no more than the surface. When it comes to the foundations of the work of reading, rather than theory, one must rely on pre-theoretical intuition and accumulation. It is like the performance by masters of a craft. And of course, it requires aptitude, talent, and tireless effort. I zealously devoted myself to this task of deciphering texts and to constructing a history of thought on the basis of that. I have a certain pride in these artisanal skills. It has been a few years since I acquired these skills; in the meanwhile, I have found a stable profession, and I live an albeit meager life with my wife in a nook in Tokyo. I think that should be enough to satisfy.

However, truth be told, while concentrating on these abstemious duties, I was not too far away from the worlds of philosophy, literature, and religion. But there were no issues for me because my focus was on Buddhist documents. To put it simply, I protected myself using philology as if it were a cage, cowardly though it may be, and thus avoided having to enter directly into the world of philosophy, literature, or religion, able to run circles in their outskirts in relative safety. It is a stupid story, really.

In that quote alone, I have exhausted half my life story. When I wrote this, I had just published *A Theory on the Formation of Kamakura Buddhism*,[2] continuing from the book based on my doctoral dissertation, *Research on the Buddhist Thought in the Early Heian Period*.[3]

2. 『鎌倉仏教形成論』 [A theory on the formation of Kamakura Buddhism] (Kyoto: Hōzōkan, 1998).

3. 『平安初期仏教思想の研究』 [Research on Buddhist thought in the early Heian period] (Tokyo: Shunjūsha, 1995).

I had finally acquired a certain amount of perspective on the history of Buddhist thought in Japan. I was placed in charge of the lectureship for Japanese Buddhist History in Tokyo University. But that was originally the lectureship founded by Tamura Yoshirō, who had mentored me. And so, as its second generation, I had the task of making this lectureship grow roots in its early phase. That was a reasonably heavy load, and I had this sense of relief that I had managed to carry it out. I could just leave things to the next generation.

At the same time, also in 1998, I published *Reading the Blue Cliff Record*,[4] and was able to share my perspective on how to read Zen books. My book *Dismantling Words and Worlds* was somewhat peripheral—a collection of essays about philosophy, religion, and literature that, as it were, were appended to my academic research. To be honest, I was not consciously trying to express any new directions of my own.

The few years after, which would mark the end of an era and the beginning of another, comprised a period of agitation for me, when I was madly groping in the dark. Thinking that I had accomplished what I ought to, my research hit a dead end and I fell into a midlife depression, constantly thinking about death. But on the other hand, while up until then I could get by merely closed up within myself, I was pulled into the surface without regard for my consent, and I had more opportunities that required me to say something. What happened was, as I wrote in the "Afterword" of the Shinsho edition of this book, "Since a few years ago, I started working with researchers from philosophy, ethics, and other cutting-edge contemporary fields in things like collaborative research projects." And in that, what had the most impact was when Iwanami Shoten's "Twenty-First Century Research Group" invited me and I joined their ranks. The debates of the eminent intellectuals at the forefront of that period were so different from my world that I felt uncomfortable, and I had no idea how to express

4. 『「碧巖録」を読む』 [Reading *the Blue Cliff Record*] (Tokyo: Iwanami Shoten, 1998).

these strange ideas I had inside. I hit a standstill. I had to express these things somehow, and this impatience stoked me from the inside.

Back when I was a student, I did somewhat have an interest in contemporary philosophy and thought, but afterwards, I ended up drifting very far from that and secluding myself in the world of classical texts. When I emerged almost 30 years after, I was surprised how much the problems of the present had changed. The courageous, politically-centered thought of the 70s—from orthodox Marxism to the new left—had completely vanished, and the main problems were issues like social recluses, NEET (not in education, employment, or training), and youth stuck in a moratorium stage of development. The spotlight was finally shining on social misfits, dropouts who could not stick with a positive sense of values—people like me. It was, unexpectedly, an easier world for me to live in. With things this way, perhaps even I could have something to say.

Simultaneously, this also spelled the end of the overriding necessity to catch up with and overtake western modernity. As usual, on the surface, the world of ideas had remained west-centric. But that too seemed to be certain to fall into an impasse. There was a strong possibility that the old eastern or Japanese thought and religion, which I had been earnestly devoted to, but which also had previously been mocked as old-fashioned, would make a comeback. And so I followed my gut and began the work, in a trial-and-error fashion, of constructing a new theory by referring to eastern and Japanese thought and religion—particularly Buddhism. The preliminary results of this took form in this book. Ever since its publication, I have been slowly developing its ideas further. I wish to refer to those developments later on.

In the process of laboring to construct my own way of thinking, it became clear that although one may refer to "Buddhist thought," one cannot merely base oneself on a commonsense factory-made interpretation of it. I had to re-rinse it, and pore through the texts of Buddhist thought myself. This implied putting the modern Buddhist understanding to question, for such an understanding relies on previous interpretations. From there, it then became necessary to explicate modern Buddhist thought. Shimaji Mokurai, Kiyozawa Manshi, D. T. Suzuki—modern Buddhists who are famous in some parts, but had yet to be afforded proper academic research. Going through their works once again, I realized that on one hand, their ideas are very fresh and there is much to learn from them, but on the other hand, if I did not criticize them, I could not construct a new way of thinking. It was especially Kiyozawa's thought that exerted a large influence on my idea of the other, particularly his interpretation from the point of view of how one should relate with Buddha as an other.

By rethinking modern Buddhism in this way, one is also able to approach modern Japanese thought anew, which is usually discussed sans Buddhism, and uncover the distortions of Japanese modernity. A reconsideration of Buddhism is at the same time a reconsideration of modernity. The criticism of modernity in Japan has been raised through the angle of postmodern thought, but this angle lacked a firm foundation upon traditional thought, and thus ended as merely a superficial trend. A genuine critique of modernity is only possible by directly grappling with tradition.

In this way, from my fumbling about, I had to face up to the task of examining Buddhist thought within the framework of Japanese modernity. In recent years, research on modern Buddhism has become quite brisk, but back when I first started working on it there were almost no required readings on it and I had to go by a series of trials and errors. The results of these were compiled in a three-volume series called *Modern Japanese Thought: A Reconsideration*. I am particularly referring to the first two volumes: *On Meiji Thinkers* and *Modern Japan and Buddhism*,[5] which were the preparatory works preceding *Buddhism vs. Ethics*.

5. 『明治思想家論』 [On Meiji thinkers] (Tokyo: Transbyū, 2004); 『近代日本と仏教』 [Modern Japan and Buddhism] (Tokyo: Transbyū, 2004).

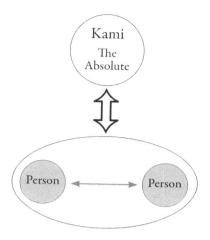

Figure 1. The Christian Worldview

Through this chronology of events, I finally managed to publish *Buddhism vs. Ethics*. However, of course things did not conclude with that. Rather, this book was the starting point of a new project—bringing Buddhism out into the field of modern philosophy and ethics and rethinking it. Next, I shall look back on the central philosophy of this book, while touching upon the developments of my way of thinking after this book.

THE PROBLEM OF THE OTHER/DEAD

When I published *Dismantling Words and Worlds*, I had yet to directly take up the problem of the dead, but the germinal form of the prototype of what was systematized in *Buddhism vs. Ethics* had begun to take shape. Especially in Part I of the former book, I proceeded from the dismantling of the linguistic world in Zen to the relationship with the other who cannot be grasped by explanatory language. I then tried to read the relationship with the Buddha as other in the first half of *The Lotus Sutra* (the gate of traces). This approach became the foundation of the development after that. As a person who

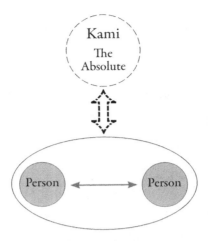

Figure 2. The Modern Worldview

has difficulty with interpersonal relationships and tends to be a recluse, but at the same time feels anxiety at the prospect of total self-confinement, the problem of the other has always weighed on my mind.

Furthermore, in the last chapter of Part I of *Dismantling Words and Worlds*, I took up the problem of evil in Shinran, and I concluded that the notion of evil in the secular and ethical dimension found in the *Lamentations of Divergences* and the religious notion of evil in the *Kyōgyōshinshō* are problems that are on different dimensions. That is not to simplistically suggest separating ethics and religion. Rather, it is my own pressing concern. Given that we are drawn to things that secular morality would most definitely reject, how should we think about this shadow that cannot be rectified by the right? From there, I proceeded to think about the religious dimension and how it differs from ethics. This too would be a problem inherited by *Religion and Ethics at Odds*.

In the transition between these two books, the biggest development lay in my discovery of the dead. One cannot experience one's own death; it is always but a limit situation (De. *Grenzsituation*). As long as one is alive, one cannot arrive at death. This brings to mind "The Paradox of the Tortoise and Achilles," where according to this philosopher's logic, no matter how quick Achilles may be, he could never catch up with the slow-gaited tortoise. However, if they actually compete (although that in itself is impossible), Achilles would surely overtake the tortoise. It is the philosopher's unrealistic theories that are off the mark, and we need to take our point of departure from the fact that Achilles does overtake the tortoise.

In the same way, although it may be said that, "So long as one is alive, one cannot arrive at death," death inevitably comes. If you cannot see this as a problem, then your theory is off the mark. Perhaps one will argue that it is impossible to talk about death because they who have experienced death cannot speak about what comes after death in the ordinary language of experience. Actually, modern philosophers all thought this way, and this resulted in the eviction of the problem of death from the province of philosophy.

If this is so, how can we take up the problem of death? Thinking about death over several years, I concluded that although one cannot experience death, the death of the other is something everyone has experienced. The relationship with the other does not necessarily end with death. If relationships ceased entirely with death, there would be no need for funerals. Buddhist memorial services (conducted periodically after someone's death) would be meaningless. And it is not just these rites that show this continuity. I think a person who has experienced the death of someone close actually feels this continuity of the relationship with the dead, even after his or her passing. Perhaps this is merely a problem within an individual's mind, but the psyche is not just imagining these things arbitrarily. I think many people have experienced the possibility of conversing with the dead in a way that is not just an illusion or an auditory hallucination. If this is so, then it is possible to properly problematize the relationship with the dead as an other, as an experiential fact. Perhaps we *ought* to concern ourselves with this.

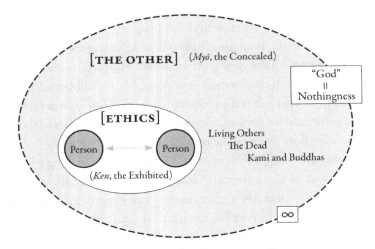

Figure 3. Worldview based on Japanese religion

With the establishment of this point of view—the relationship with the dead as an other—the core concept of this book was completed. It was largely shaped by the impulse drawn from the psychiatrist Watanabe Tetsuo's *Death and Madness*,[6] but there were other moments that overlapped in order to form this book. Another big formative event was my encounter with the religious culture of the Tōhoku region, which maintains a rich relationship with the dead. Also, I had been able to interpret the first half of *The Lotus Sutra* as a theory of the other, and so I found a novel perspective of seeing the Buddha as one of the dead, in my tackling with how to interpret the latter half (the main gate) of that sutra. This perspective opened up a way to reconsider the entirety of Buddhist history. This comes from the realization that if Mahāyāna Buddhism develops from the main presupposition of being *after* Buddha's death, then one can say that it is none other than *the Buddha as one of the dead* that sets the basis of Mahāyāna.

6. See page 172, note 5.

In the process of dealing with the notion of the dead head-on, funeral Buddhism—which had previously been belittled and avoided in Buddhist scholarship—can be seen as a new task. It is funeral Buddhism that has carried on the most active relationship with the dead. There are many problems with it, and we cannot simply accept it as it is. But at the same time, we cannot discard it as an inauthentic form of Buddhism. It must be said that from the point of view of understanding Buddhism, it is of utmost importance to properly evaluate the role that funeral Buddhism has played.

As we have seen, this book's theoretical core lies in seeing the opening of the problem of the other in the place transcending the domain of ethics as *ningen*—the betweenness of persons—and placing the dead as the archetypical other. However, the domain of *ningen* as the inter-personal and the domain of the other that transcends that are not unrelated. It is in the tension that binds both wherein religion is born. I also think that, rather than seeing Buddhism as a stereotyped theory, Buddhist thought needs to be re-contextualized within this tensional relationship.

THE DEVELOPMENT OF THE THEORY OF THE OTHER/THE DEAD

After this book, I took it as a starting point and worked to deepen its theories and reconsider them within the domain of the history of thought. I deepened and developed these theories in *The Other, the Dead, the I* and *Philosophy Live: A Perspective from Japan*. And in works like *Reading Buddhist Scriptures, Late Premodern Buddhism* and *The Modernity of the Other/Dead*,[7] I brought these theories back to the

7. 『他者/死者/私』 [The other, the dead, the I] (Tokyo: Iwanami Shoten, 2007); 『哲学の現場』 [The site of philosophy] (Tokyo: Transbyū, 2012), English translation: *Philosophy Live: A Perspective from Japan*, forthcoming; 『仏典をよむ』 [Reading Buddhist scriptures] (Tokyo: Shinchōsha, 2009); 『近世の仏教』 [Late premodern Buddhism] (Tokyo: Yoshikawa Kōbunkan, 2010); 『他者・死者たちの近代』 [The modernity of the other/dead],

history of thought and considered them from there. I shall not go into an in-depth discussion of these works. Rather, I would like to touch upon the theoretical developments after *Buddhism vs. Ethics*, focusing on the parts that connect to its philosophical core.

First, I began to use the words *ken* (exhibited, bright, clear) and *myō* (concealed, dark). *Ken* refers to the domain of ethics as the "betweenness of persons," and in contrast to that, *myō* refers to the domain of the other that cannot be grasped entirely within the domain of *ken*. This is not just a problem of terminology but signifies my use of the methodology of history of thought to connect contemporary problems to the medieval period in Japan. This contrast between *ken* and *myō* can be found in the medieval Buddhist Jien's history text, *Jottings of a Fool* and also in medieval literature like the *Heike monogatari*. It thus links to the characteristics of the medieval worldview.

According to Jien, people think that people (*ningen*) move history, but the truth is not what it seems. For example, the relationship between the imperial family and the Fujiwara-Sekkan houses is by no means by chance. Rather, it is due to the contract between Amaterasu, who is the ancestor of the imperial house, and Amanokoyane, who is the ancestor of the Fujiwaras. In this way, the history of the human world of *ken* is steered by the movements of the world of *myō*, which transcends the world of *ken*. Jien sets seven stages for the development of history, and the first stage is the harmony between *ken* and *myō*, wherein the principle of the Way holds sway as itself. In the second stage, the principle of the Way of *myō* gradually shifts, and the people of *ken* are unable to understand it. In the third stage, what the people of *ken* see as the principle of the Way no longer accords with what the invisible hosts (the inhabitants of *myō*) think.

As we see, in Jien's view of history, the human world of *ken* gradually drifts away from the world of *myō*. It was not just Jien who thought this way. A Buddhist Shinto thinker from the Northern and South-

---

Kindai Nihon no shisō: Saikō, vol. 3 (Tokyo: Transbyū, 2010).

ern dynasties period in Japan (1336–1392 CE) named Jihen further developed this idea and came up with the theory that can be said to be representative of the medieval view of history. In this theory, history begins with a period when myth and history were one, but these two gradually drift apart. This is in some way similar to the modern view of history where, through this separation, a purely secular human history becomes possible. But while the modern view sees this as progress; in contrast, the medieval view of history saw this as a degeneration, wherein the human world of *ken* loses touch with the world of *myō*. As we see, the terminology of *ken* and *myō* were widely used in the medieval period. In Shinto, *yū* (secluded, deep, as in the aesthetic ideal of *yūgen*) is used instead of *myō*, and they can be combined as *yūmei* (usually meaning deep and strange, the other world) which is often used.

By adopting vocabulary that has this sort of background and referring to the domain of rational ethics as "*ken*," I have tried to break free from rationality, and thus refer to the world indecipherable by reason as *myō*. Against this, one might say that I could have just used "the sacred" and "the profane"—terminology from religious philosophy that has been in circulation for a long time. But in the case of the sacred and the profane, the former has a nuance of being something divine, at a higher dimension than the latter, and ultimately tends to be taken up by the monotheistic idea of God. In contrast, the world of *myō* or *yū* is not necessarily on a higher dimension than human beings. It includes of course the dead and ghosts (*yōkai*), but also, to put it in Buddhist parlance, it includes the hell beings and hungry ghosts that transmigrate across the six realms. Because of this, it does not quite fit the idea of "the sacred." Because of this, rather than "the sacred" and "the profane," I think it is *ken* and *myō* that are more appropriate for ideas based on Japanese tradition.

However, the historical concepts of *ken* and *myō* are not necessarily identical to the concepts I am trying to employ. In its historical usage, *ken* and *myō* have the property of differentiating domains of existence. Human existence belongs in the domain of *ken*, and in the domain of *myō* we have non-human, also invisible beings. In contrast, in my usage, the otherness of the other is always according to the way it relates to the self. Thus the area of *myō* does not exist in itself. Even fellow human beings, so long as they can understand each other are included in the area of ethics as the inter-personal, and can therefore be called *ken*. But if these same people fall into a relationship where mutual comprehension is impossible, this aspect of being an *other* that deviates from ethics comes to the fore, and can be thought of as part of the area of *myō*.

The second development after *Buddhism vs. Ethics* was that I started using schematic diagrams to express the structure of the world that I had in mind. I include three figures here. The first two figures are very simplified representations of the western worldview. Figure 1 illustrates the Christian worldview, as it was received in Japan, where the living have a relationship of "love of neighbor" with their fellow living beings. That world of the living was created by an absolute being—God—and is emplaced within a relationship with God. However, in such a schematic representation, it is difficult to envision the relationship between the world of the living and the dead.

Figure 2 is the modern worldview that moves from the previous Christian worldview to the experience of the "death of God," where the verity of the absolute being/God is disputed and the world of the living is seen as self-sufficient. It is within this view that the scientific worldview was constructed, and we can think of materialism as the extreme form of this way of thinking. However, I overly schematized Figures 1 and 2, and the actuality of the western worldview, particularly the Catholic worldview, is more complicated. Rather, a more appropriate way to put it is that *Japanese* modernity took up the western worldview in this schematized form.

This fact had a decisive influence on the modern Japanese view of Buddhism. With the coming of modernity to Japan, Buddhism was placed as one of the *shūkyō* (religions). *Shūkyō* was originally a Buddhist term, but in the modern period, it became the set translation for the word "religion." In that process, Shimaji Mokurai of the True Pure Land Hongan-ji sect played a leading role, and restricted the notion of religion to problems of faith within the minds/hearts of human beings. Through this restriction, he aided in the establishment of religious freedom, into which politics (which is in charge of externalities of the human being) ought not intrude. This led to the realization of the separation of religion and the state. That was a critical accomplishment, upon which the modern Buddhist thought of Kiyozawa Manshi and others unfolded.

Their religious views fundamentally adopt Christianity as a model and interpret Amitābha similarly to the monotheistic notion of God. Because of this, their worldview is similar to Figure 1. Furthermore, Zen opposed Pure Land Buddhism and was widely taken up by intellectuals. Zen was talked about as something other than the western model of religion. But fundamentally, it was understood as a rational worldview similar to Figure 2. For the most part, the Buddhist understanding of the philosophers of the Kyoto School is largely split between Figures 1 and 2.

However, we cannot completely grasp the actual form of Japanese Buddhism through either of these figures. What were left out? These figures rejected elements like funeral Buddhism, Esoteric Buddhism, Shinto and Buddhist syncretism as premodern, irrational, impure elements that are not part of authentic Buddhism. This effectively sealed off and erased the abundant world in which the dead, the kami, and the countless buddhas act. However, for many people in Japan, this world is real, and many people still live within such a worldview.

I have consistently criticized "philosophers" who trample underfoot worldviews that are natural to us, only to forcibly and heteronomously impose ill-fitting worldviews in their place. Against them, I have emphasized the need for a path that expresses the most natural worldview in a way that anyone can understand. In *Buddhism vs. Ethics* and the succeeding works, I have been trying to seek out precisely how to express such a worldview. It ought to be possible to find a place for the dead, the kami, and the buddhas, who tend to disappear in worldviews like Figures 1 and 2, through a worldview of ethics and the other, or *ken* and *myō*.

I have tried to express the worldview based on Japanese religion through Figure 3 on the following page. I depicted the world of *ken* as an ellipse, wherein the relationship between persons is regulated via ethics. It has a rather limited, narrow scope. But outside of it, the expansive domain of the other, *myō*, spreads out. In actuality, it is better to see the world of *myō* as encompassing or overlapping with *ken*. The reason why I deliberately placed *ken* and *myō* horizontally from each other, rather than vertically, is that the absolute being and human beings are not in a hierarchical relationship. It is better to grasp the world of *myō* as in the depths of the world of *ken*. Rather than proceeding skyward, it is better to visualize it as going deeper into a forest, seeking out its depths. It is because of this that I previously argued that "the sacred" is not an appropriate way to express the world of *myō*. Furthermore, the gap between *ken* and *myō* is vague and fluid, rather than clear-cut.

Incidentally, there are some thinkers who argue that monotheism is militant and that polytheistic religions are religions of peace, and the Shinto nationalist standpoint has anti-monotheistic propaganda. I think this is unforgivable. Monotheism and polytheism are on different dimensions. In Figure 3, the God of monotheism can be placed as the extreme limit of the world of *myō*. That is a yonder shore we can never reach, and because of this, must be said to be a "nothingness" (*mu*) inexpressible by ordinary language. Therefore, polytheism does not reject monotheism, but rather, monotheism can exist side by side with polytheism, albeit on different dimensions.

Figure 3 expresses this worldview. Of course I have expressed it two-dimensionally for the ease of understanding, and it does not grasp the whole picture. However, with this figure, this worldview can be expressed, to a certain extent, as an image. Provisionally, I refer to this as a "worldview mandala."

THE MANY LAYERS OF OTHERS AND
THE ELASTICITY OF THE SELF

As we see above, I made some progress ever since this book, and I have expressed these ideas in several books. From here on, I would like to write a little about what I have been thinking about these days. I have shown these ideas to discussants but I have yet to develop them sufficiently. There are two main points here. First, can we not think of the *myō* domain of the other, not as disorderly, but as having a multi-layered structure arranged by depth? I have expressed this idea somewhat in "Aiming toward a New Philosophy."[8] Second, about the relationship between the *I* and the other, rather than seeing the *I* as able to establish itself by clearly drawing a boundary line, can we not see this boundary line as vague and unsettled? I spoke of this idea briefly in Chapter 18 of this book, but after, I pushed it further in Chapter 4 of *Philosophy Live*.

As to the first point, as I show in the figure, the *myō* domain of the other is a mix that includes the living other, the dead, kami, buddhas, and other "others." Perhaps some might argue that because these beings transcend the grasp of human reason, it is pointless to think about some order to this world. However, there are natural differences in their way of relating with us, and through that, it is somehow possible to think of layers. At present, I have provisionally divided this domain into three layers.

The first layer is comprised of the living other people as "other." Amongst those who are other to us, the living are the closest to the domain of comprehensible ethics, and everyone necessarily encounters the living. The other person straddles both the domain of comprehensible ethics and the domain of the incomprehensible other. The realm of ethics presupposes that individuals are autonomous as individuals and act on the basis of rational judgment. Within this realm, the

---

8. Sueki Fumihiko, 「新しい哲学を目指して」 [Aiming toward a new philosophy], *Fukujin* 16 (2012).

subject is established within law and ethics. Nature, in so far as it is grasped scientifically and understood as abiding by rational principles, would fall into this domain.

However, interpersonal relationships are not necessarily rationally constructed. There is no way for me to know what is going on inside another's head, and the other is fundamentally incomprehensible. Even in relationships, prior to reason, things are often swayed by emotions that are beyond rational control.

Not only that, I myself am actually an incomprehensible other. If I do not have medical tests done, I do not know how my body is really doing. Even matters in my own psyche are mostly beyond my control. The self itself is the nearest other.

In this way, when thinking about contemporary human and social fields like medical care, nursing, caregiving, education, childcare, and even politics, the recognition that the self and the other are comprised mostly of other-like (or "alter") elements is of utmost importance. The genuine connection between self and other can only begin when we let go of the arrogance that oneself and other people can be understood entirely through reason.

The second layer of "others" is comprised of the dead. Even though one cannot understand a living other, one can try to make sense of the other by feel and can come into contact with him or her. In contrast, while the dead were once living and we were able to come into contact with them, in the present it is no longer possible to relate with them directly. While the living go back and forth within the realms of *ken* (ethics) and *myō* (the other), the dead do not enter the realm of *ken* and are thus completely other—their existence is vague to that extent. While there is the standpoint that acknowledges the existence of the dead as souls, the standpoint that sees death as turning into nothingness is also legitimate. However, even if one takes the latter standpoint, one still has to have some sort of relationship with departed loved ones. The case of the dead typifies the cases wherein what matters is not existence but relation.

If one takes this sort of approach to the dead, funerals and acts that "comfort the spirits of the dead"—issues that have been hidden and refused in philosophic discussion—can be taken up directly. One can find new angles to approach things like grief care, for after all, one can only discuss the problems of terminal care and the aged if one bears in mind the ideas of death and the dead. Furthermore, by recovering the relation with the dead, we can take up the problems of mass death from war and natural disasters directly, and we can re-account for the world of the living from a new angle.

In the third layer, deeper into the dimension of the other (*myō*) than the dead, we have kami and buddhas. As one goes deeper from the first layer to the second and to the third, the individuality of existents becomes more diffuse and direct contact becomes more difficult. Even more than the dead, one cannot find an answer to the question of whether kami and buddhas "exist" or not. The stance that these do not exist at all is perfectly possible. This would mean adopting a worldview like Figure 1 or 2. However, even so, one could not deny that there are people who live in relation to kami or buddhas. Because of this, one has to recognize that the standpoint of Figure 3 is also legitimate. In Figure 3, one can account for monotheism. And if we consider the fact that even a materialist standpoint relates with the dead, gods, and buddhas (in a negative form), such a standpoint could be placed within this schema as well. However, if one takes the stance of Figure 1 or 2, there is no space to accommodate people who have a worldview as in Figure 3. Because of this, conceivably, it is Figure 3 that has greater inclusivity and applicability.

As we see above, we can see the *myō* domain of the other as having three layers, and discussing the problems by layer can be said to reduce confusion and increase productive argumentation.

The second point I wish to discuss is that the limit separating self and other is not necessarily clear. The region of inter-personal ethics comes about through clear stipulation, and the differentiation between self and other can be well-defined. The most formalized expressions of that are systems of law. However, once you actually relate with the other, the boundary between self and other becomes unstable. As I wrote in Chapter 18 of this book, the domain of the self cannot be so clearly fixed. For example, if one tries to express one's individuality through clothes and accessories, such an expression also becomes part of the self. What then if one wore other clothes? Furthermore, if one's own psyche is beyond one's control and is thus other, what might we even call "self?" In other words, this thing called the "self" cannot be substantially defined.

The link between self and other also easily tightens to the point of fusion. "I" becomes "we." The most typical example is that of sexual relations. If the self were a self all throughout, then in the sexual act, a man and a woman (or two people of the same sex) would merely enjoy their own separate pleasures. One's partner would merely be a means for the self to feel pleasure. That seems far removed from actuality, does it not?

In this way, "self" is fluid, identifying and differentiating, assimilating and dissimilating from the other. Assimilation eliminates the difference between self and other and aims at the two becoming one body, whereas dissimilation creates a barrier between self and other in resistance. These movements simultaneously move in different directions, and as the self blurs its boundaries, it moves fluidly like an amoeba, and there is no way to grasp it.

This indeterminate way of being of the self is necessarily caused by its existing in relation to a non-rationalizable other. As this relationship proceeds deeper into the second layer, relating with the dead, and deeper still to the third layer, relating with kami and gods, the self is faced with the threat/wonder of a more total loss of selfhood.

For example, when thinking about issues in fields like medical care, nursing, caregiving, childrearing, or education, there are many problems that are unresolvable if we see the self and the other as completely cut-off from each other. Does it not make it easier if we see the relationship of self and other in the fluid movements of assimilation and dissimilation? These sorts of issues need to be more frequently discussed in depth from here on.

HISTORY OF THOUGHT AND PHILOSOPHY

As I have mentioned, I was able to delve into the problems of this book by taking a step back from preexisting philological histories of thought. However, that does not mean throwing out the considerations of history of thought. Rather, what I have done in this book is an attempt to disassemble certain aspects of traditional Buddhist thought and then reconstruct them. Furthermore, the terms *ken* and *myō* that I introduced after this book keep in mind a connection to previous Japanese thought.

If we are to construct new philosophies in Japan, then just as western philosophy faces contemporary problems while dialoguing with the history of ideas, Japanese thinkers also need to proceed forward while at the same time seriously considering the past ideas of Japan. The fields of history of thought and philosophy need to progress in parallel, with a back and forth movement between them. However, this basic task has yet to be accomplished. I myself often thought within the framework of Buddhism, and did not sufficiently consider things with perspectives like premodern Confucianism and *Kokugaku* (National Study / Revival) in mind. My book, *Late Premodern Buddhism*, somewhat took these into account and I began to glimpse the directionality by which I could make sense of the flow of the history of thought.

Furthermore, and quite unexpectedly, in 2011 I was nominated to be the chairperson of the Japanese Association for Comparative Philosophy. I felt compelled to reflect once again on the methodology of comparative thought, which I had not thought much of previously, and develop my ideas accordingly. Japanese thought first took shape through interacting with other cultures as "other," (although this is true for philosophies everywhere). A history of thought that is isolated within one country would never come about in the first place. Today, in order to construct history of thought and philosophy, it is indispensable to grasp this fact in a self-aware manner.

Awareness of these issues has led me to be quite interested in trying to resituate my ideas within the history of Japanese thought. I have yet to adequately put my ideas together, but allow me to list some problems that I am wrestling with now.

First, within the framework of Buddhist thinking, it is necessary to recapture the issues in the history of thought in the formative phase of medieval Buddhism. A theory centered on Kamakura new Buddhism used to be widespread, and thinkers like Hōnen, Shinran, Dōgen, and Nichiren were taken up as if they were isolated great thinkers, all the while ignoring the others. However, the categories of *ken* and *myō* were never restricted to a small number of thinkers (like those above) to begin with. Rather, these categories imply a rediscovery of the spiritual-historical foundation that formed the medieval way of thinking. If so, I think medieval Buddhist history of thought cannot proceed by connecting the dots between isolated thinkers, but rather must be understood as such an expansive, large-scale flow.

From this point of view, I am currently very interested in the development of Esoteric Buddhism in the mid-Heian period (the whole era spanning 794–1185). I think that the theory of the five wheels of Kakuban (1095–1144) is of grave significance. In this theory, the world is formed by the five elements of earth, water, fire, wind, and void. These are expressed in the shape of a square, circle, triangle, half-moon, and jewel. Stacked from the bottom to the top, these make the five-wheel pagoda. Each is symbolized by a sacred Sanskrit character, and the five also express the five organs of a human being: liver, lungs, heart, kidney, and spleen. In this way, through the mediation of the five wheels, the truth of the world and the body of the human being are unified, and this means becoming of one body with the world of the Buddha. Another way to put it is that the entirety of the world is condensed within this body, and that is none other than the realization of the world of the Buddha—attaining Buddhahood in this body/life.

This sort of conception of the theory of the body began in a prior period, and its great significance lies in the fact that it tries to grasp the human being not in an abstract way but as a concretely embodied existence. Zen and *nenbutsu*, which developed after, originally took this sort of a conception of the theory of the body as a point of departure.

Furthermore, attention to the human body deepened the thinking about the issues surrounding sexual activities between man and woman, and the fetal development and childbirth that proceed from that. This sort of attitude was particularly significant in that, together with the doctrine of *hongaku*, it tried to give Buddhist meaning to the way of living of human beings as it is. However, this way of thinking was referred to as "Tachikawa tradition" and treated as a heresy, preventing it from receiving due acknowledgment.

Furthermore, this theory of the five wheels has important implications for the theory of the dead. Even prior to former, there were memorial services for the dead, but the development toward funeral Buddhism, beginning with the practices of burying corpses, began here. On the basis of this philosophy, a corpse is seen as on par with the body of the Buddha, that is the origin of the world, which is why the five-wheel pagoda is meaningful as a gravestone. Medieval Buddhism, even the movement called Kamakura New Buddhism, was formed on the basis of this sort of foundation.

Toward the end of the medieval period, a new worldview and view of life and death were introduced with the coming of Christianity. The previous worldview developed horizontally, as we see in the notion of the "Western Pure Land of Amitābha." In contrast, Christianity brought in a vertical way of thinking wherein the absolute being exists in "heaven." (This is consistent with the Confucian way of thinking that developed in the late premodern period.) Also, in the view of life and death in Christianity, there is a strictly maintained either/or between heaven and hell—a view very different from that of Buddhism.

Confucianism originally possessed a very rationalistic way of thinking, which if carried to an extreme, would result in the denial of existence after death. However, in order to emphasize ancestor worship, a complete negation of the afterlife could not be fully carried out. In Japan, Confucian formats for funerals and ancestor worship were not adopted, and all of these were carried out in a Buddhist fashion. Because of this, Confucian ways of thinking did not sink in completely, and they exist in a multi-layered fashion with Buddhist views of the world, life, and death.

Against the ambiguities of such views, new challengers emerged in the form of the novel perspectives of *Kokugaku* and Reform Shinto. Motoori Norinaga attempted to elucidate the ancient Japanese worldview prior to the coming of Buddhism, on the basis of the *Kojiki*. But he was not able to sufficiently expound on the view of the next world (or afterlife). Norinaga's disciple Hattori Nakatsune published *Three Great Ideas*, in which he schematically represented the process of the formation of the world through 10 stages and divided this world into a structure with three layers (seen vertically): heaven, earth, and the underworld (*yomi*). Heaven is the domain ruled by Amaterasu—the sun. The earth is the region where human beings live. The underworld where the dead go was originally seen as being beneath the earth, but ultimately was thought of as the world on the moon ruled by Tsukiyomi. Norinaga's *Commentary on the Kojiki* included *Three Great Ideas* as an appendix, showing Norinaga's approval of this worldview.

Hirata Atsutane took *Three Great Ideas* as his basis but tried to put important changes. Atsutane wrote *The True Pillar of Spirit*, which, while citing the former book, rejected the idea that the dead go to the underworld. He argued for a novel view of the next life, wherein the dead do not go to some underworld separate from our world, but rather, stay here in our world, close to us. Here, he presents a noteworthy, new view of life and death wherein the vertical worldview is rotated once again, and the world of *myō* is seen as on the same level (but on the reverse side) of the world of *ken*. Therefore, the dead are not cut off from the living, but are placed within a relationship with the living even after death.

The Reform Shinto of the Hirata School was eventually widely supported and became the main driving force of the Meiji Restoration. But despite that, with the dawn of modernity, it was seen as old-fashioned and cast out. Shinto was restricted to state rites as State Shinto, and its free activities became constrained. The problem of what comes after death was carried on by funeral Buddhism, but because it did not fit with modern rationalism, it was evicted from the surface layer of the discourses of the world, and people stopped actively discussing it. Amidst that, Yanagita Kunio's *Talk of the Ancestors* clarified the view of life and death seen in the general populace (see Chapter 27 above), and this can be seen as a successor of Atsutane's views on life and death. Furthermore, philosophies that actively recognize our relationship with the dead do come up here and there as isolated cases, as seen in Tanabe Hajime (who I discussed in this book) and Uehara Senroku (who I take up in *The Modernity of the Other/the Dead*). But for a long time, these philosophies were seen as oddities and were left buried in dust.

Above, I have broadly examined the history of Japanese thought centered on the issues of the view of life and death and the theories of the dead. Seen in this way, the history of thought of Japan's past is by no means old-fashioned. I think one has seen that it contains many hints to help us elucidate the latest contemporary problems. Scholars of the history of thought and those of philosophy have been kept apart. Even within the former field, specializations have been divided according to period and school (like Buddhism or Confucianism), and woefully lacked a way of thinking that would dare to integrate these divisions and cross swords with contemporary philosophy. I insist that it is the urgent task of today to go beyond this overspecialization and construct a new philosophy and a new history of thought.

Index

Made in the USA
Monee, IL
18 July 2024

62143863R00152